Klondike Paradise

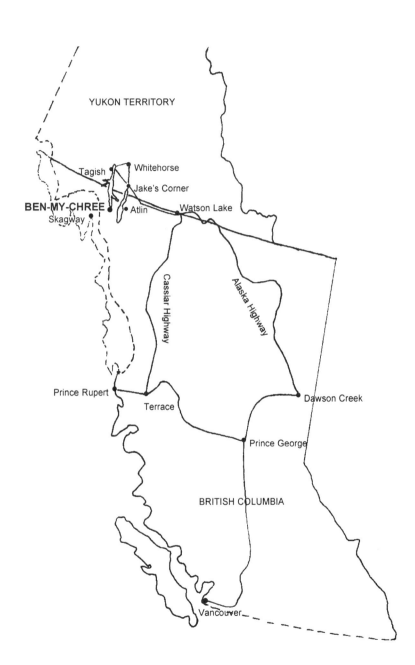

Klondike Paradise

Culture in the Wilderness

by
Cy Porter

With a Foreword by
Pierre Berton

hancock
house

ISBN 0-88839-402-0

Cataloging in Publication Data
Porter, C. R. (Cyril Robert), 1920-
Klondike paradise

ISBN 0-88839-402-0

1. Porter, C. R. (Cyril Robert), 1920- 2. Tagish Lake Region
(Yukon)—Biography. 3. Yukon Territory—Biography. 4. Ben-
My-Chree (Yukon) I.Title.
FC4049.T33Z49 1997   971.9'102'0922   C97-910517-X
F1095.T33P67 1997

Editing and Production: Nancy Miller and Sharon Boglari

Published simultaneously in Canada and the United States by

HANCOCK HOUSE PUBLISHERS LTD.
19313 Zero Avenue, Surrey, B.C. V4P 1M7
(604) 538-1114 Fax (604) 538-2262
HANCOCK HOUSE PUBLISHERS
1431 Harrison Avenue, Blaine, WA 98230
(604) 538-1114 Fax (604) 538-2262
email address: *sales@hancockhouse.com*

Contents

Dedication

I humbly dedicate these writings to my extended family whose encouragement and labor made possible a record of Ben-My-Chree: Helen Patricia Porter, Kerrie Helen DesRosiers, Dennis Alan DesRosiers, Stephanie Vivian Gould, Kim Wilson Porter, Cheryl Lee Porter, Russell Robert Porter and Arlene-Fay Porter.

Published with the assistance of the Canada Council.

Photographs are acknowledged, unless from the author's collection, by photographer, collection and archives, using the following abbreviations:
YA—Yukon Archives, Whitehorse
HC/YA—Hegg Collection/Yukon Archives
WH/YA—McBride Museum Collection/Yukon Archives
DSC/YA—Dennett-Selfer Collection/Yukon Archives
ADC/YA—Reginald Brook Collection/Yukon Archives
TC/NAO—Taylor Collection/National Archives of Canada
ALHLC/YA—Alaska Historical Library Collection/Yukon Archives
TSC—T. S. Laudon
GB—George Raithby, courtesy David Raithby & Marion Brook
GM—G. M. Taylor, courtesy late George Simmons, Carcross
GMT—G. M. Taylor/Atlin Archives
BC/YA—Bratfold Collection/Yukon Archives
AHSC/YA—Atlin Historical Society Collection/Yukon Archives
FCS—Foto Craft Studio, Whitehorse
JAG—John A. Gould, Dawson
NAC—National Archives of Canada
DD—Dennis DesRosiers

Acknowledgments

A host of generous men and women have helped me set down this true story of Ben-My-Chree, but none more than her and our children to whom I dedicate. Helen Patricia, my wife of more than fifty years—everyone calls her Pat and seems to love her—took my dream on faith, structured and nourished it with constant support, and like all wives who give more than they seek to receive, she has shared the joy of birth and growth of her husband's vision. To her and our eager and excited sons and daughters, I owe it all.

Close at hand too, are real Yukoners, genuine humans who leave their minds open like groceries on the cabin shelf or kindling in the log-cabin oven. Pierre Berton, the one-and-only, he of school days and Monopoly fame I can never forget. No other will ever come near his northern authorship. No one should try. Suffice to know him, to admire, to bask a little in the sound of his voice on telephone and television now and then, and to perhaps be one of the few who are privileged to know that Victoria boy scout face—the real Berton—peeking impishly up through type lines in his *Drifting Home*. He introduced me to Yukon. We traveled north together in 1938. I will ever be grateful.

Bea and George McLeod, who by turns wondered and worried about we greenhorns, never ceased to be there when we needed them; their dock sheltered our boats and their lovely log home at Tagish always had doors wide open. On their land rested our vehicles year after year at the end of a long Alaska Highway jaunt up from "Outside." When we purchased Ben-My-Chree in 1971, they launched their own boat and saw to it we were guided safely through shallow channels, around hidden rocks and into historic harbor at journey's end—true citizens of Canada's golden territory these.

There are many others: Alan Innes Taylor—tower of a man, explorer, whaler, mountie, river pilot, soldier, author, consultant, friend—who punned his way into my heart as he gathered together the beginnings of Yukon's archives. He taught me respect and love for all the North, not just Ben-My-Chree, which he too revered.

Roy Minter, he of public relations fame, who, with pen and camera, fleshed out knowledge of the British Yukon Navigation company, part of the railway and shipping fleet known as White Pass & Yukon Route. He contributed many a glimpse into a deep personal river of wonder for things clean, clear and special up there. His moving film *There's the Land. Have You Seen It?* is both a classic and a prize-winner. Lately his splendid book *The White Pass—Gateway to the Klondike* marries creation of a miracle railway to the discovery of gold, detailing the almost unbelievable engineering feat which pierced the mountains from Skagway, Alaska to Whitehorse, Yukon, opening up a vast wilderness to prospectors, settlers and commerce. Roy has gone now. We miss him.

A special family, Reg. Jr., Marion and Jim Brook, proprietors of Brooklands Wilderness Camp, contributed in large measure to our enjoyment, appreciation and understanding of Ben-My-Chree. Their warm and hospitable log home at the mouth of Rupert Creek, eastward a little from Golden Gate on Graham Arm, became our last stop on lake journeys from Tagish River to home port at Ben-My-Chree. Reg passed on a few years ago. He was a pioneer patriarch. Marion and Jim carry on. Jim recently founded Osprey Air. With two airplanes, he keeps busy coming and going like the swallows that nest under Brooklands' eaves. There will always be only one Marion, charming hostess, chef, amateur taxidermist, generous to a fault. She often dropped in at Ben-My-Chree by boat or plane, loaded down with fresh vegetables, big smile, much laughter and a couple of hugs.

Many visitors brought items and memories to our wilderness door as we struggled to preserve Ben-My-Chree and all it meant to our family, and to those who preceded us. Forgive me if I do not name them all. They came by the score: by boat, kayak, canoe, inflatable and airplane, even landing in our garden by helicopter. Some had known the founding Partridges; others, having heard of their hospitality, made their first visit, sitting in garden or cabin and reliving with us the wonders of a special place.

Their names appear in our visitors books, check-by-jowl with similar older records, where names by the thousands lie in Yukon archives. Apart from the famous and well-known ones, here is a name that stands out. When I was a scoutmaster in Duncan after

WWII, my district commissioner was Colonel Doppinq-Hepenstal, a veteran of the South African conflict. His delight was to doll up in Zulu warrior gear: brown shoe polish from head to toe, lion-mane headdress, rattles on wrists and ankles and a menacing assagai (spear) stabbing round the boys' campfire as he wildly chanted. The boys loved him. So did I. In May, 1922, his name appears in one of the visitors books at Ben-My-Chree!

I want to accord a special word of appreciation to the Principal Archivist and staff in the Territorial Archives at Whitehorse. All were consistently courteous, providing photographs, a full copy of Kate Partridge's diary and, most precious of all, data which strengthen a personal link with the Partridges.

I wish all who helped a happy reward if they recognize their contribution within these pages. If they do, then mayhap they will share with our family the hope that the Partridge creation at Ben-My-Chree will never be forgotten while still a clean, cool breeze wafts down from the glacier at valley head, passes softly over their homestead, and stirs the Tagish on West Taku Arm.

Foreword

When I was in my teens growing up in Victoria, B.C., in the decade of the Great Depression, my closest friend was Cy Porter. I didn't call him Cy or even Cyril. I called him Hambone, which is what everybody in St. Mary's Boy Scout Troop called him. We met as fellow scouts and we rose through the ranks together, becoming King Scouts, Patrol Leaders and, later, Rover Scouts. Cy was the leader of the Owl patrol; I was leader of the Seagull patrol; in those days it was scouting and not high school around which our lives revolved.

We were both fanatical hikers and campers. Every Sunday, no matter what the weather, our two patrols met at the scout headquarters in Oak Bay and hiked off from the end of the tramline to Thetis Lake or Elk Lake or Beaver Lake. It didn't matter if it rained or snowed, there we were in our short pants and yellow slickers, often cowering under a bridge in the rain to cook beans and bacon. Sometimes we two were the only ones who turned up, but we went anyway. Some of my brightest memories are of those marvelous outings.

In the summer of 1937, thanks to my father, I got a job in a mining camp in the Klondike. The following summer I planned to go back again and my father thought there'd be a job for Cy as well. The Klondike was one of the few regions in Canada—perhaps the only region—which the Depression hadn't struck. Gold is gold, bad times and good. There were jobs to be had if you could get North. However by 1938, so many men had gone to the Yukon to get work that the jobs started to run out. Cy and I were getting ready to go when my father wired that there'd be a job for me but not for him.

There are moments when a single decision can change the course of a man's life. For Cy Porter, this was one. Should he trash his plans or should he go anyway—on spec? He didn't hesitate. "I'm going with you," he said. And that altered his entire future.

He didn't get a job in the mining camps of the Klondike but he did get work on the stern-wheel steamers—the last of their kind—that were still puffing their way from the silver mines of Keno

10

Hill down the turbulent Stewart River to the Yukon. His account of that period in his book is a valuable piece of social history. For Cy was very much a part of a vanished era when the stern-wheeled steamboat was king, when the splash of the scarlet paddlewheel and the hoot of the steam whistle were familiar sounds, and the whole world seemed to run on birch wood.

Cy and I saw very little of each other in the years that followed. I went off to UBC. The war intervened. I moved East. It was not until 1971 during a visit to the Yukon that I heard his name again. I was in Whitehorse and was talking with some Yukon friends about Ben-My-Chree, the garden spot of the North, a name so magical it caused old-timers to sit up and smile. It was known not only for the luxury of its famous gardens, but also for the hospitality of its owners—a watering place *par excellence* for the tourists who went out of their way to visit it and remained to be charmed.

It saddened me to hear that it was no more, that tragedy had overtaken its owners, that the warm-hearted couple who had held open house there had died, and that Ben-My-Chree was empty. But then someone said, "Did you hear that it's been purchased?" I hadn't. "Some guy from British Columbia bought it for his family," he told me. I asked the name. "It was Cy Porter," he replied.

Cy Porter—a name from the past! I couldn't have been more delighted. Knowing my old friend, I dropped my concerns about the future of Ben-My-Chree. It was now in good hands.

I thought then about how we are all effected by life's accidents. Cy Porter became a Yukoner after he heard my stories of the North in the Boy Scouts. His decision to go North was the same kind of decision my own father made when, on the spur of the moment, he left Saint John, New Brunswick, in 1898, and joined the gold rush. The North changed his life, as it was to change Cy's life. Ben-My-Chree became for him and his family a kind of anchor, and in acquiring it, and digging out its romantic and sometimes tragic story, he has provided us with a valuable footnote to history.

PIERRE BERTON
KLEINBURG, ONTARIO

11

Introduction

Since his earliest beginnings, man has relied upon a power greater than himself. Often recognized is a destiny which seems to enliven, enrich and mold each phase of life. From earliest childhood (some of which was not hugely happy), I have sensed what many describe as a great Good. Not until middle life, through the stirrings of personal fate, does a conviction that He has something in store beyond the ordinary become recognizable.

I first saw Ben-My-Chree in 1938, as a waiter on *Tutshi* out of Carcross. It was a traumatic experience. Massive beauty assailed the eye. In company with a crowd of passengers, I managed to see for myself what brought these world travelers so far afield and away from civilization. The combination of domestic flowers, mountains, river and lake, plus the hospitality worked its magic. Otto and Kate Partridge, founders of what they called "an international oasis of peace in the wilderness," had passed on in 1930, but a wise transportation company had maintained their tradition. As a young chap of eighteen I was smitten. With boyish enthusiasm I made myself a promise: come what may, I would own Ben-My-Chree one day.

What follows speaks of lives beyond the ordinary, lives before my time, and a little about the Porter family. We have come to perceive our comings and goings in Canada's northland as an abundant, continuing gift. My wife, my children and I have received mental and visual joy as a result of our northern travels. We are grateful. This book is an effort to share some of these gifts with you.

"Along the trail," as Yukoners casually remark when describing their lifestyles, have marched the names of famous adventurers, surveyors, prospectors and pioneers. The closer to the poles one journeys, it seems, the more outstanding they become. Many Yukon pathfinders achieved renown because of Klondike, the world's most famous gold rush. There had been many rushes to various parts of the world before, but none ranked in intensity or numbers of men and women than this frantic charge through wild barriers against odds which render latter-day gambling comparatively risk free.

The truth is that few early prospectors, long in these northlands, staked and recorded claims from which they dug vast quantities of the yellow metal from river banks and hills, becoming rich beyond imagination, gambling and gamboling fortunes away as gaily and grandly as they had initially answered the call of the wild. Only after these first fortunate searchers had made their way back over tremendous distances to cities such as Seattle and San Francisco, bearing ragged suitcases, canvas bags and animal skin pouches full of gold, did the lightninglike fever strike worldwide. Almost overnight men from all social levels and occupations of life downed tools and careers, abandoned home and hearth, and with little or no knowledge or experience of the perils and terrors awaiting, set out on a quest which could not be denied. They came in the thousands, frantically searching for what they fervently believed would be personal bonanzas, placing them high above their fellow man. Their search meant facing flesh-searing cold, blizzards of snow, blindness and even death. Despair was their constant companion; starvation marched close behind.

How did these ordinary men and women accomplish such amazing feats of spirit and strength? What was it that enabled them to meet challenges which today cause men to stand in awe? Is the answer that they rose to such heights of accomplishment simply because the challenge was there and circumstances demanded they perform, and in order to survive, they could do none other?

Consider the "Klondike kings." Their names at one time rang from the Yukon's hills, echoed from bank to bank across a thousand creeks and rivers: George Carmack, Tagish Charlie, Robert Henderson, Skookum Jim, Big Alex McDonald, Dick Lowe, Max Endleman, Bill Gates, Charlie Meadows, Antone Stander and Belinda Mulroney. Their adventures were astonishing, their deeds, fabulous. Yet how many of these mighty Eldorado names are remembered today? Do mountains, rivers and lakes stand as monuments? Not many. One can visit the Yukon community of Carmacks; Tagish Charlie lives on in lake and river. Pierre Berton, Canada's recorder of Northern history, keeps before us these kings in his classic book *Klondike*, but there are few names on our maps to mark the passing of these golden people.

Not of such men is my yarn. They have their chroniclers. Libraries of volumes—some true, some not so—trumpet triumphs and disasters, immense deeds and self-inflicted suffering, and seek to justify the search for riches, finding a crock of gold at rainbow's end. In two short years the rush for Klondike came and went. "The tumult and the shouting" (Rudyard Kipling, *Recessional*) died. 1898 passed and with it Dawson's thousands abandoned Yukon's first capital for the beaches of Nome, Alaska. The wild-eyed masses pressed on, still searching, if not for gold, for a triumph to enrich their lives. Alas, their dreams, their personal will-o'-the-wisp ever receded over yet one more hill, 'round another river bend.

Today, in a world where instant communication overloads the mind, where scientific expansion shrieks and roars in and out the station of our intellect—as did the steam trains of our youth—there may yet be the chance and time to climb a personal Chilkoot, to look about and appreciate a neighbor's affection, fears and afflictions, to recognize another's contribution to our personal happiness or success.

Let us journey to lonely land I know.
There's a whisper on the night wind, there's a star agleam to guide us,
And the wild is calling, calling...let us go.
Robert Service, *Call of the Wild*

The place known as Ben-My-Chree began with a search for gold. That was the prime incentive. In the end however, what was discovered, what remains an indestructible monument to human endeavor, was not the tantalizing metal, but treasure infinitely more precious: the gift of a couple's example to others. Two unique lives were fully lived. With the living, a generous spirit was colorfully bestowed upon fellow men and women. So remarkable was the gift that it reached out across the world, embracing surprising numbers of people, many rich and famous. Like Bonanza's pilgrims, Ben-My-Chree's visitors were seeking something. Their experiences deserve to be remembered.

To some, the adventure may not seem significant. Others, particularly those who have turned their footsteps north in more recent years, feel a special consciousness steal upon them when they drive

14

the Alaska highway, step out of a jet in Whitehorse, or see Skagway and Chilcoot's peaks from a cruise ship's rail. A fortunate few may even behold Ben-My-Chree, learn a little of what happened in that sand-beached valley where precious memories are still guarded by a glistening glacier.

Principal players on this wondrous stage acted out a life which miraculously came to be inherited by our family. My story is a record of the past, and a little of our own times as we strove to relive bygone historic and hospitable days. We came to believe Otto and Kate Partridge, the original founders, contributed something particularly valuable, not only to their neighbors and the somewhat limited group of Yukoners who knew them intimately, but to a surprising number of worldly people who visited briefly.

Long after the day of their departure, visitors realized they had been exposed to an experience which somehow lingered and continued to enrich their minds in a manner strange and wonderful.

In 1938, only eight years after the Partridges had died, I first beheld their home and learned of their lives. It was obvious their fame had spread afar. As the years came and went, their homestead at the head of a lake was written about in newspapers and magazines. The McBride Museum in Whitehorse exhibited a few of their personal belongings, diaries and letters. A short mimeographed summary about Ben-My-Chree was passed out to visitors. There were many Yukon citizens who, having visited and loved the Partridges, somehow felt a vested interest in this beautiful wilderness. Although most of the old-timers are no longer about, there are still a few whose faces break into delightful smiles the moment "their place" is mentioned. And each year more courageous visitors hear the words "Ben-My-Chree" and find their way south on Tagish Lake.

We acquired Ben-My in 1971. Since then we have spoken to many who visited and have heard of the effect it had upon their lives. We have taken many photographs and shown color slides in lecturing various audiences. Always the reaction is the same. There is excitement, wonder, a little sadness and requests for a detailed account. So here it is. My hope is that Girl of My Heart will continue to be beloved, for it is living history, an oasis in the wilderness, a personification of the North's golden rule.

Chapter 1

Into the Country

Because those picturesque white ships played such a leading role in my Yukon adventures, they deserve to steam right into the story of Ben-My-Chree. If it had not been for the flip of a card in my game of chance, the opportunity to go to sleep under northern lights with vibrations of power and wonder from a pounding paddlewheel, it is unlikely Ben-My-Chree, Manx-Gaelic language from the Isle of Man meaning Girl of My Heart, would ever have entered into my vocabulary.

Back in 1893, a very early sternwheeler, the *Yukon*, struggled upriver from St. Michael in Norton Sound, Alaska, toward Fort Yukon where the Porcupine River joins that old Hudson's Bay fort at the Yukon River. So primitive and game-filled was the country in those days that Frederick Schwatka, an early-day Yukon explorer and surveyor, wrote that a pioneer paddlewheel steamer "could hardly make a voyage to old Fort Yukon and back without encountering a few herds of these animals (moose) swimming across the stream, and exciting were the bouts with them, often ending in victory for the moose with the *Yukon* aground on a bar or gravel."

Aksala was my initial signpost. She was one of several wheelers whose decks I came to know intimately. Each ship had a beauty and character all her own. Those tall shallow-draft ships, steam and hot cinders spurting from yellow funnels, were so much a part of the country up there. Nothing could compare with the wailing whistle when such a vessel was still out of sight around a river bend. Then majestically she hove in sight, bow-wave thrusting against river current, gold-lettered nameplate sparkling on high atop her pilot-house. She might have been pushing a barge or two, but from the colored house flag on her bow mast to thrashing scarlet wheel astern, she represented romance to all who beheld her. She stood for all the North. A Bulkley Valley pioneer and historian, once part owner of a Skeena River sternwheeler, thus described his ship:

> In sight and sound a sternwheeler chugging upriver has been likened to a steam locomotive. Like a locomotive most sternwheelers used noncondensing engines; that is, the steam, instead of being put through condensers and used again, is discharged right into the smoke stack. This serves the purpose of giving the fire forced draft, making It possible to burn any kind of wood, wet or dry.

> This was the reason, too, that a sternwheeler bucking current, could be heard for miles since the steam exhausted into the stack with a roar. The sound was similar to a steam locomotive leaving a station, except that locomotives used a valve that allowed steam to escape all at once, producing the characteristic puff-puff-puff, A sternwheeler used a slide valve that allowed the steam to escape more gradually, making a long screeching sound, something like phew-phew-phew.

> On the whole, a sternwheeler was a pretty noisy contraption. In addition to the steam screeching from the stack, there was a continuous slap-slap-slap as each bucket on the paddlewheels hit the water. The vessels had a deep-toned baying type of whistle which frequently added to the uproar. Then, if everything wasn't going right the mate or captain would contribute a lively selection of comments, thus adding a personal note to the din.

To me, a sternwheeler slapping her way through white-water rapids, spray cascading from bow and paddlewheel, steam and smoke belching skyward in great swirls of black and white was a picture that once seen was never forgotten.

Back then, *Aksala* was my whole world. Between her decks upstream on the Stewart River was transported provisions, fuel, freight, rail and a few passengers—the very life of Yukon. In 1938, there were about a dozen such ships serving Yukon and Alaska on river and lake, although immediately before, during and after the Klondike gold rush, the number of ships reached an astonishing 250. My ship, and two like her, carried me that season. They were exclamation points in an era now all but forgotten. It is still possible to board *Keno* as she lies hauled onto the river bank at Dawson, fully restored as a tourist site. *Klondike* also has been freshed up by the federal government and put on display in Whitehorse. In Fairbanks, Alaska, an actual steamer operates, carrying visitors during summer months; but she is not a working vessel. Her owners valiantly try to provide a glimpse of bygone days. Those with questions and cameras know the journey is not for real, but at least they catch a glimpse of glory.

Occasionally a private entrepreneur takes a stab at renewing river traffic. Tied to the river bank in Whitehorse is an aluminum craft, which takes tourists downriver to Dawson. Modern and comfortable, she provides knowledge of Lake Lebarge, following in the wake of the great ones such as *Klondike, Casca, Dawson, Whitehorse* and many more.

Down south on the Mississippi, others seek to relive past days when they were honored by the presence of those like Mark Twain, while a Dixieland band thumped away in the background and gamblers fleeced the gullible. I never saw gambling on Yukon's ships during the 1930s, but perhaps I was on those concerned more with commerce, less with chance. Probably in addition to Dawson's Klondike games, early steamers saw gold dust pokes pass from hand to hand, while dancing girls smiled seductively and helped things along.

Once my wife and I briefly cruised the bayous of New Orleans with friends from Toronto. Neither the ship nor the slow-moving murky waters throttled by locks, were in any way akin to my beloved North. Normally soft and warm like a southern belle's shoulders, Louisiana temperatures that year were strangely rough and raw. Rain and wind drove us indoors. We played desultory bridge to pass the time, ignoring bland views, wishing for a hotel and hot shower.

In the North, the year 1938 still spelled adventure. Canada's territories sang a siren song in spite of a desperate depression.

Everyone talked and lived what we called the dirty thirties. As a young chap of eighteen, to be where gold had been discovered and where sternwheelers like *Aksala* (Alaska spelled backwards) were still alive, was a wonder of wonders.

I arrived in Whitehorse early in the spring in company with friends from Oak Bay, Victoria: Pierre Berton and Bill Drury, son of a partner in Taylor & Drury, one of Yukon's pioneer merchants and fur traders. Bill popped back into my life again in 1968 during my stint as Centennial Commissioner. I rented a car from his service station in Whitehorse.

Pierre's father, a mining recorder in Dawson, had somehow managed to find us both a job. We were to drive steam pipes into the frozen tundra ahead of gold dredges. Just before we left, we learned Berton's job was assured; mine had evaporated.

I joined a group of four other unemployed that first night, bedding down by a warm lobby stove in the old Whitehorse Inn. Next day we found out about a Sleepy Hollow shack, about a half-mile walk through the snow. The price was right—$5 a month. As always, you get what you pay for; it was no bargain. Wall planks had shrunk, and if there was a wind, which was often, snow blew between the cracks. We named it House of Many Wallpapers. I used to squirm about in my sleeping bag on the freezing floor, trying to get warm, wondering where an early owner had found dozens of wallpaper samples which bridged some cracks and crannies.

Cash was short, but we managed by get by for a few days on rice pudding and raisins, porridge and tea *sans* milk and little sugar. Two of the group landed jobs in the shipyards where sternwheelers were being readied for the season. Three of us began digging a basement. The ground was frozen, but we were shown how to build a little fire, shift it about from time to time, then hack away with pick and shovel at the partly thawed ground. By day's end we resembled worn-down chimney sweeps, sooted and muddied about. But twenty-five cents an hour was good money and meant food.

Later when the job ran out, I took to the streets, knocking on doors to inquire if there was need for some expert spring cleaning. One of my calls was upon a Mrs. Watson, a kindly lady, mother of Tom and Fraser, who happened to be Boy Scouts, like me. That helped. She put me to work washing walls and ceilings, salary the same, two-bits an hour, but including dinner. I ate at 11 A.M., just before her husband Bill Watson, Chief of the White Pass & Yukon commissary, came home. I was well across the living room ceiling when he arrived, grumbling over his lunch. It appeared a waiter, hired in Vancouver for the steamer *Aksala* had developed appendicitis, so an otherwise full crew was short a live body. Down the ladder I scrambled and stuck my head through the kitchen doorway.

"I'm sorry, sir, but I couldn't help overhearing your problem with staff. It just so happens I'm the best waiter you ever saw, and you don't have to get anyone from Vancouver. I'm here!"

"Is he a good worker?" asked Watson.

"Yes he is," replied Mrs. W. "And another thing. He's the hungriest young fellow I've ever seen!"

"You've got about half an hour to get your gear laddie, and get down to the dock. There's a plane headed for *Aksala* in LeBarge Slough. If you want the job, get moving!"

I moved alright, running all the way to Wallpapers and back to the plane. That night, replete with white shirt, bow tie, jacket, trousers and tea towel over the left arm, the profession of steward welcomed a new recruit. I had not the slightest idea about waiting, polishing silver, disinfecting toilets, making beds or shining long linoleum corridors, but the salary was $50 per month plus full and plenty. Fellow waiters took pity on my ignorance, and with the benefit of urgent need I became a quick learner. Full and plenty meant all I could eat and a cabin with clean sheets all to myself. Paradise!

By break-up, when winter ice was thawing, beginning to shift in sloughs and move slowly downriver, *Aksala*'s crew was working as a happy team. One morning we cast off her lines, steam hissed, giant pistons moved back and forth, and the scarlet sternwheeler began slowly to turn. We were off downstream on the storied Yukon River.

The duties of a waiter at that stage were not arduous. No passengers, only the officers to care for. One can only shine corridors and polish silver so much and with no beds to make, I found time to watch the first "wood-up" (the loading of cordwood from the river bank), experience a hair-raising swoop through Five Finger Rapids and marvel at sounds only a sternwheeler can make.

Five Fingers was the last major obstacle on the Yukon River before Dawson. Having weathered Lake LeBarge, where fierce storms could erupt with little notice, and successfully navigated constantly shifting sand and gravel bars, steamboat captains now faced the most dangerous part of the river for boat navigation. The immense rushing body of water sought to force its way through restrictions created by four islands in the river forming five channels. An ominous roar arose, to which a steamer now added bow wave, thrashing sternwheel, the snarl and swoosh of hard-pressed machinery and the howl of steam exiting under forced draft from her funnel.

A ship en route upstream kept to the east channel, the safest one. Here a scheme was devised to bring boats through. A greased cable was anchored above the rapids in a building. When a wheeler arrived at the channel, the cable was taken aboard and wound round her winch. She was literally pulled through the rapids. Going the opposite direction, downstream, she was held back, sternwheel pounding full-speed astern.

In any early dawn I sometimes stood at the stern, high on the upper deck, looking down and back along our rolling white wake. Below, the wheel thumped and whooshed, echoing from river banks. Myriad swallows darted back and forth in and out of nest holes on the golden sand banks.

Aksala was my first love. By the thirties she had passed her prime, relegated to hauling freight up the Stewart River to Mayo, returning downstream with Keno mine silver ore to Stewart city where the mighty Yukon mingled waters. Barges loaded three sacks high with silver-lead ore were transferred at this point to mainline steamers bound upriver for Whitehorse at railhead.

Sometimes I pause nowadays, set aside whatever is of moment, press a memory key and retrieve in motion, sound and color *Aksala* in all her glory. Little of her lives today. In the sixties she was hauled out onto the highway just south of Whitehorse and shoved up on a few crumbling timbers, pilothouse askew, funnel gone. Nothing restorative was done to her. She began to slowly fade, like a lonely actress, once famous on the world's stage, sadly remembering golden times when men adored her beauty and fawned at her feet. Presently someone erected a sign proclaiming the birth of Paddlewheel City. A little later another sign warned: "Keep Off!" Soon the rotting hull disappeared, perhaps for firewood. At that stage my feelings were beyond hope. I simply refrained from looking at her last resting place whenever we drove into Yukon's capital.

Said the late Captain Ken McLees in *Alaska Magazine*:

> The best fate for a sternwheeler is to die in harness. If they are hauled on the beach they follow an inevitable pattern. First they start falling to pieces, then come the souvenir hunters, then the vandals who strip them. It is a sad end. They should be dismantled immediately or else preserved, for once they're gone, they can never be replaced.

As the days passed on *Aksala* I came to know each officer and crew member. Officers consisted of the captain, pilots, three mates, first and second engineer, purser and chief steward. We held food court three times a day, but from time to time Captain Ewen "Hughie" Morrison would call down for a flagon of tea, which was duly hand-delivered to the pilothouse, on high. At mealtime, forever hovering unobtrusively on the table perimeter was our nemesis, the chief steward. Never will we three waiters forget him. On the surface he was debonair, suave and charming. That was the face he presented to officers and the few passengers who graced *Aksala*'s run. But beneath was a sad soul, finicky, sometimes unfair. He was not a man to easily love.

When *Aksala* first welcomed me, I managed to survive mainly because of brotherliness of fellow waiter Bert Weatherall. Bert had been a waiter for many years, journeying up each season from Victoria. He was everything the chief was not: generous, kindly, helpful, humorous, a real friend and genuine human. He never tired of easing my trial. He taught me to write orders on the palm of my hand when stage fright froze all memory during my first few meals. Of course, on *Aksala* using an order pad was simply not done. Besides, there were no pads.

Bert explained how to outwit the chief, who had a repertoire of sadistic habits. According to Bert, cabin passengers came in three classes: those who slept lightly and fastidiously, hardly ruffling a sheet; those who turned and moved about in bed a little; and those who slept like a live earthquake, tearing the hell out of everything!

In making up a bed for those in the first category, it was necessary only to tighten up things a little, slap on a fresh pillowcase and call it quits. Number two required a couple of additional refinements, primarily to obliterate any marks made by a passenger on the bunk-side. This was accomplished by judicious application of a tailor's chalk ball. Since it was the chief's habit, born of many year's experience, to pass his blue serge arm down the bed border, one found it imperative to stand backside foremost to the chalk mark, so preventing "the nemesis" from making a full pass.

One day, fifty years later, I was visiting one of my real estate salesmen in a Victoria hospital. He had cancer. As I walked sadly out of his room, I saw a little, old hunched-up man slouched in a wheelchair parked in the corridor. I had to walk past and as I did, I glanced at his face. The years dropped away suddenly; I stopped and grabbed his hand.

"Bert!" I cried. "It's you, isn't it?"

The face, lined and gray now, looked vaguely up at me. Then slowly it began to change, to bloom all the way into a smile.

"I know you," he said, "but I can't seem to put a name to it; a little slower these days y'know."

"It's Cy from *Aksala*!" I cried.

"Man, oh man, is it really you?" asked Bert.

It was. We chatted a few precious moments, remembering by-gone days on the Stewart River; then a nurse came and wheeled him away. I later learned times were difficult for Bert. His memory was fading. He had ceased northern treks some years previously, and retired. His principal reason for living had been to coach a young boys' English football team. After a time he could no longer do even that. His health failed and with it, his spirit.

When training my real estate salesmen, I always insisted they strive to be givers. I tried to instill in each the idea that the more you give of yourself, the more you surely receive. Bert Weatherall was a giver. Would that they have signed him on to an eternal steamer, perhaps as chief steward.

As the season progressed, summer sun melted snow high on Yukon's peaks. Water levels rose, but when snows were mostly gone, the Stewart River ran shallower. Rumors of transfer to a

23

smaller ship began to circulate. We learned only two waiters were needed on *Keno*; that would leave me out in the cold.

During off-duty hours on *Aksala* I had made a habit of typing invoices for the purser just to keep my hand in from business college days. My reasoning was that one day this sojourn in a Northern paradise would come to an end. City smells, perhaps unemployment, would be my lot. Having made a good friend of the purser, I sought him out and asked his counsel.

"Not to worry, Cy," said he, "*Keno* has a deck boy vacancy. I've stuck your name down for it. You get a ten dollar raise, too. It's rough, but you'll get used to it. Here's a bunch of invoices. Jump to it!"

I jumped.

There were some pluses and a few minuses on *Keno*. No more private cabin, just a humble lower berth aft the engine room, hard up against the ship's stern wall where water cast up by the paddlewheel smashed and boomed. Within a few feet of my head a huge piston shaft hissed back and forth as it drove the paddlewheel. To begin with, the noise was like taking up residence inside a train engine. A cloud of wet steam enveloped my bunk. Most of the time when I went to lie down, the covers were clammy. They say one can get used to anything. After awhile, particularly after a hard wood-up, my weary bones did not mind any conditions. In fact, ever since those days I have been able to sleep anywhere, anyhow.

Engines have always been fascinating to me. *Keno*'s machinery was special. During off-duty hours I often watched engineer Fred Vey caring for what he called "my babies." He would lovingly polish brass pressure gauges, gently oil large and small moving parts and adjust valves minutely. Each motion indicated affection and respect, as though the gleaming machinery was somehow alive. Great wheels, pumps, shining shafts seem to reciprocate Vey's care.

Whenever our ship's wood supply dwindled, the whistle blew a few short blasts and we put into the river bank and made ready to wood-up. Here hundreds of cords of four-foot pine were piled close to the river. A contract to cut wood for the sternwheeler's boilers was one of the prime means of augmenting income for trapper-prospectors in steamer days. One, sometimes two of these hardy souls, guided by steamer needs, would build a log cabin and start a woodpile. With axes, arm-powered (arm-strong) cross-cut saw and dog-team locomotion, long stacks were built up to feed the hungry boilers. In *Aksala* on the Stewart, twenty cords could be burned every eight hours on the upriver run to Mayo.

If the bank was high, or the river low, we manhandled heavy wooden trestles ashore and set them up at regular intervals. Then we mounted steel-tipped ramps on top, each ramp with six-inch walls. Two "deckies" (deckhands) manned two-wheel freight carts, while their comrades took turns loading from woodpiles on the bank. Each cart carried about half a cord when piled high. Down the ramp a load would roar, the deckie riding the handles of his cart, maneuvering one wheel at a careful angle against the ramp wall, causing a braking action. On the ship's deck he would make a crucially timed sharp right, never slackening speed, shooting down alongside the boiler where I waited to help dump the load. There was barely time to pile up the round cord wood before the next load arrived. We took on about a dozen cords, sometimes more, and by the time all was stowed, this deckboy was about done in.

Now and then woodpiles were burned over by a forest fire. The logs were black with soot. Add to that heat from the boiler, clouds of mosquitos and "no-see-um" flies, round logs which refused to stay piled the required eight feet, noise and sweat, and you have the picture.

On wood stops we would occasionally see, and sometimes meet, one of those rugged individuals who cut wood for the steamers. Woodcutters, like many loners found along those rivers, owed their existence to the White Pass & Yukon Route fleet. Winter trapping augmented their earnings, but the appetite of sternwheelers made it possible for them to count on regular cash each summer.

One day upstream when the steamer was burning close to a cord an hour against a stiff current, we put into the shore to take on another jag of fuel. Unlike *Keno*, when I was a waiter on *Aksala*, there was not much to do when wooding, so I gathered up some local mail, climbed the bank and walked up to where the woodcutter was sitting in front of his log cabin. Like most men who live alone, he quietly studied me as I came closer. It was as though he customarily waited for events to occur in his life rather than charging out to meet them.

"Good morning!" I said.

"Hmmm," he replied, smiling through a fine crop of whiskers.

"You been here long?"

"Yep."

"Been at it for years, eh?"

"Yep."

"Nice dog."

"Old."

"I bet he's a good friend."

"Yep."

"Well, so long."

"Yep."

Two letters, a few newspapers and four copies of *National Geographic* offered clues to an earlier life Outside. I often wondered what lay behind calm visages like these. Year after year they hand-cut wood by the hundreds of cords, apparently content with companionship from a sled dog or two. Except for steamer calls and the occasional Indian moving about, a woodcutter went for months without speaking to another human. He seldom quit the job, carrying on for years, sometimes disappearing without a trace. At other times one would be found dead in his lonely cabin when the season's first steamer came round the bend.

In Whitehorse once, as a barber cut my hair, I asked him why people came to Yukon. "Well, son," he said, "some of 'em are running away from something; others from someone. An' some of 'em are just here to make a buck!"

The longer I stayed up there where the wind blows cold, the more I came to know that barber was close to the truth.

When deckboy on *Keno,* one of my daily tasks was washing down the ship's deck rails. No cinder screen graced the funnel in a sternwheeler's draught system. Every ounce of power was needed to ensure maximum steam production. Red-hot wood clinkers spewed out, more so when the ship was straining upstream against a freshet. Lifeboats had metal covers to protect their wooden interiors against fire. Deck rails received several coats of fire-resistant paint. My job was to sweep up the clinkers and wash what seemed to be miles of yellow wooden rail tops where steam smut regularly marred their appearance. It was an endless job. No sooner was one portion sparkling than wind or vessel changed direction and down came the enemy. Now and again a large cinder would take aim at the back of my neck where shirt met skin. There was "a hot time in the old town" while I yelled, hopped frantically about and peeled off to get at the little devil.

In spite of those minor problems, to see the river bank passing by was the stuff of great adventure. Game was abundant. At times we saw moose, caribou, bear, coyote and even the rare glimpse of a wolf.

As deckboy on *Keno*, I was designated to the bow of a lead barge as we moved swiftly downstream. I used a long sounding pole measured in feet, alternately marked red and white. With it I measured the river, shouting depths back to the pilot high aloft. Sometimes we came round a bend and ran smack into a herd of caribou. There was no stopping in that swift current. We passed right over the animals as they struggled to cross, drowning many. If our cook was awake, he would rush to a stern loading door, longshoreman's hook in hand. With help from pantryman or messboy, he would lean out and gaff an animal. The meat was yarded aboard, hung for a day or two and served to all hands. An immediate joy was liver, one of the tastiest Northern treats. We seldom traveled at night, so there was plenty of time to fish for trout or grayling. The country was full of rabbits and sloughs teemed with geese and ducks. We roamed about during the evening with a .22, determined to vary the ship's menu.

The most terrifying duty on *Keno* was running the ship's steam winch, located close to her bow. At different sections of the Stewart River we encountered rapids. Upstream journeys required lining whenever the volume of current exceeded our best speed. At such times we put into the river bank and picked up a greased cable anchored at top and bottom of a rapid. The line lay loose, enabling a few loops to be passed round the winch wheel. Slack taken in, we cast off, and with every ounce of steam crowded on, paddlewheel thrashing, swung out into the rapids, literally hauling ourselves inch by inch up the maelstrom.

So strong was the rush of river, we hung out there, swinging from bank to bank, cable singing like a taut banjo string. A crew member told me it was not uncommon for a strand, or the whole cable, to snap. When that happened the line became executioner, screaming down upon our deck with force sufficient to cut a deck beam, or a man, in two. The mate pointed to a three-foot square hole just in front of the winch. "If she snaps," he said, "just dive headfirst in that hole. There's a mattress about four feet down."

Fortunately, a few years previously I had passed a boy scout fireman's badge, which included diving off a trestle onto a mat, doubling up on contact to avoid a broken neck. Diving over that winch into a black hole was a shade more daring, but cables held during my watch.

Winch duties included another challenge. Upriver usually we pushed one or two barges loaded with assorted freight and machinery. Skill was needed to exactly curve those barges when rounding a river bend. The corner had to be navigated to permit just the right volume of river current to sweep down against the outer side of barges and ship. Too much turn would cause the connected vessels to veer into the right river bank. If the river was wide at that point, blocks and tackle were snapped like cotton thread, flinging barges against the ship's side, forcing her broadside to the river, and so onto a gravel bar or island downstream. Too little turn swung barges and ship to the left with similar results. Someone higher up kept an eye on me in those days, and upon the mate likewise, because we managed to avoid those horrors.

The ship, however, was not always lucky. One day, while pushing two barges heavily laden with ore sacks downstream, one of the deckhands snapped his sounding pole. It took but a moment to grab a replacement, but that was long enough for his barge corner to touch on a hidden gravel bar. In a second we were amidst crashing planks, a whiplash of dead-weight barges, a tangle of rope and blocks; the steamer slammed broadside onto a bar, smashed the paddlewheel and twisted an engine piston.

Apart from tremendous pressure of water on our upstream quarter, we were in no immediate danger, but we soon learned this was not the best of steamboat accidents. Getting underway again entailed back-breaking labor for all hands, day and night. All hands meant everyone. We were divided into three teams, working four hours on, four off, round the clock. Each group was headed by a mate. The skipper Hughie Morrison, so far as I could tell, never slept. He was everywhere, flashing black eyes missing nothing, roaring orders to mates, crew and anyone who seemed to slack for a second. He was "pure paddlewheel" as the old hands said.

First the ship had to be refloated and her paddlewheel repaired. A team was then put ashore with tools, much rope, blocks and tackle and peeves. They struggled through brush up along the bank, stringing light rope between themselves and *Aksala*. They cut a clearing, dug a hole and buried two short logs about ten feet deep, at right angles to each other. This deadhead, as it was called, was attached to a heavy cable hauled out from the ship. Giant gin poles, mastlike timbers, were now lowered on each side of the ship and set into river bottom. With winches grinding away, tackle straining, gradually inch by inch, foot by foot, the ship (which had been lightened as much as possible) was poled free of the bar and slacked down alongside a barge.

Every sack of ore was trucked onto *Aksala*, the first barge hauled into deeper water and reloaded. Then it was number two's turn. By the time all were floated free and the paddlewheel and engines repaired, we were all so tired we shuffled about like a group of zombies. But afloat we were and with barges maneuvered into line again, the flotilla set off downstream once more. It had taken two full days and nights. We arrived at Stewart City just in time to sweat out transfer of barges to the *Whitehorse* and then, oh joy, a full twelve hours in the sack. The skipper slept too, snoring like a trooper.

Aksala and *Keno* were disparagingly referred to by our mates on Whitehorse-Dawson mainline tourist ships as "the old ore run." Yet each time we set out for Mayo it was in expectation of more excitement and, thank heavens, no gawking sightseers who from time to time fell overboard and gave mainline skippers a case of the screaming abdabs!

We ferried survey parties now and then, men and horses, up, down and across the Stewart. Horse flies big as freight cars and no-see-ums with lances leveled, were thick early in the season. Men had some protection with broad-brimmed hats, face and neck netting, gloves and pants tucked into boots, but the horses were tormented night and day. It was not unusual for a horse aboard to go berserk, breaking free and tearing about on the freight deck, banging into walls and doorways until at last, finding an opening, leaping into the river. There was little chance of survival from water, rock or bear.

The deckboy on downstream runs faced quite a different task. I was given a flashlight, wooden mallet, several wedges, short two-by-fours and a few soft patches. Soft patches were one-foot-square wooden slabs covered with oakum and burlap, liberally tarred on the down face. When the ship scraped and thrashed her way over a gravel bar (a frequent occurrence), my job was to scramble below decks with my stock-in-trade and search for split and leaking planks.

While crawling about down there in greasy bilge with my bundle of fixings, the ship would run over yet another bar. Each time took years off my young life. There was a noise like confined thunder, violent vibration, with jets of water where least expected. Mindful of the mate's command to save batteries, I sat shivering in stygian darkness, waiting for the hiss of a leaking plank. It was somewhat like waiting to be bit in a pit of vipers. At last the bar was gone. Off we went, banging in the patches and props. My heart simply was not in it.

Well upriver was a ranch named Maisie May. Here lived an elderly farmer-cum-prospector; Maisie, his young wife; and an early son of about nineteen. They kept a few cows, raised enough hay and grain to feed them, and put in a good vegetable garden with raspberry and blackberry vines. The son was a little simple as our skipper put it. Each time we put in at Maisie May, the boy would lumber aboard, bearing an armful of vegetables and fruit and an old, red, lard pail full of milk. Our cook welcomed the fresh garden goodies. The milk was meant as a special treat for the captain. The boy bore it proudly aloft to the pilothouse. One of my duties was to attend there on these occasions, standing by while the skipper carefully thanked the lad, handed me the pail with a flourish, and commanded, "Cy, put this in my cooler. Smartly now!"

Floating on the pail's surface were various questionable items such as cow hair, hay and worse. The pail had a distinct aroma. By prior agreement between the skipper and myself, his cooler was an altogether different type of receptacle than the term usually implied.

At season's end the ranch owner was invited aboard for dinner. Each year the captain asked him whether this was the season to go

Outside. Invariably the answer was, "I don' rightly know about m'self, but Maisie may."

Who knows whether this annual conversation gave rise to the ranch name. I never did discover whether Maisie stayed or went, but the farm carried on for many years. It would be fun to launch a canoe at Mayo and drift down to see what remains there by the riverside.

When we arrived at Mayo the crew were free to longshore. Pay was one dollar an hour, good money in those days. My partner, Joe, a very large Native, was hugely strong, silent and obviously contemptuous of his greenhorn helper. Each ore sack weighed seventy-five pounds, measured about one by two feet by eight inches. Together we loaded three burlap sacks onto one of the wood trucks which I then rode down-ramp to *Keno*'s deck. This went on hour after hour until I was ready to drop. One look down on the ship at the mate, who scowled viciously at any sign of quitting, was enough to pump in a little more energy. Joe just gazed down from his lofty height, now and then offering a wide-ranging spit, but no smile or word. At shift end he looked down once more, his dark eyes taking in this sorry specimen. Then his moccasins turned about and he slowly shuffled off through the dust in the general direction of downtown Mayo.

Sternwheeler meals were terrific. Breakfast frequently meant a stack of hots six high, four or so fried eggs, bacon, butter and syrup. Toast, jam and lashings of coffee. Daily menus were prepared by the chief steward. Since we were a freighter rather than a tourister, our food was somewhat simpler. Large passenger wheelers served five-course dinners, luxury indeed in the North.

On *Keno* there was one savage personal incident. The smaller ship burned less wood than *Aksala*. But we still had wood-ups round the clock. As deckboy I had begun to harden up about midseason; yet keeping pace with truckloads of wood was still rough work. One of the deck hands had been temporarily promoted to third mate. It went to his head. He had always been a bully and now was a holy terror. Large, loud-mouthed and lantern-jawed, he delighted in standing just by the stokehold shouting ribald remarks at me as I sweated to keep the woodpile high and tidy. One day was particularly hot, dirty and fast-loading. I was weary beyond all reason. In the midst of a sooty, burned-over load, something just snapped. I

31

seized a stick of cord wood, whirled it round my head and let fly at the mate. The wood caught him just below the knees, knocked his legs out from under him and sent him head first down onto the stoker, who immediately punched him in the face.

Afterward I realized my action was anything but wise. I could have caused the mate or stoker serious injury. As it turned out the mate merely had a badly bruised leg, sore neck and bloody nose. He never harassed me again, taking up post toward the bow, well out of range. Nobody liked him, and the skipper, who took a bit of a shine to his deckboy, kept a weather eye on that mate until season's end. One other benefit was that the crew thereafter held me in some esteem.

I left *Keno* after a while, transferred briefly to *Tutshi*, once again in the role of steward. She ran on Tagish Lake, from Carcross to a strange and beautiful wilderness homestead called Ben-My-Chree, a Manx-Gaelic name from the Isle of Man, interpreted as Girl of My Heart. This was the purest of tourist runs. Once more I enjoyed the luxury of private cabin, white sheets and all.

The name of my new ship reached back into traditional ages to days when "Too-shy," originally a Native word, meant "deep, dark water." Her shapely bow would cleave the waters of Tagish, a many-armed fish-filled southern lake. First white explorers, pioneer prospectors and later Klondike gold seekers would strive to shape their tongues around "Tako" or "Tahka." They were unable to cope at all with the Native Indian name Ta-Gish-ai. When the British Yukon Navigation Company launched a graceful sternwheel steamer at Carcross on June 12th, 1917, their choice of *Tutshi* was a good one. Her owners were proud of the vessel, and said so: "She is not large. In fact you would probably call her small. But she is a perfect gem of a boatbuilder's handiwork."

In length, Tutshi was 167 feet long, thirty-five feet beam with a gross tonnage of 1,045 tons. When launched, she was capable of carrying eighty first-class passengers at a speed of thirteen to seventeen knots, generating steam by burning cord wood. Later a "Texas" (upper) deck increased capacity to 120 passengers, for whose convenience she was converted to burning oil. In 1955, she was retired to Carcross and eventually the Yukon government purchased her in 1971.

Where is she now? All that remains are a few crumbling orange planks, part of her paddlewheel, and a shadow of the once proud bow. She had made a final run from Ben-My-Chree in 1956, bearing the last vestiges of lives and legends created by Otto and Kate Partridge.

She lay at dockside for a time, then was hauled broadside up on wooden ways. Last of the lake wheelers to be beached, *Tutshi* seemed to be quietly weeping, perhaps yearning for adventuresome and exciting days when miner's boots scarred her decks, or later when businessmen and grandees viewed this awesome land from the safety of her cabins and railed walkways. Down below on her freight decks, she had hauled horses, mining machinery and pioneer supplies.

Shortly after government acquisition, sizable federal funds were set aside for restoration, so that visitors could learn of her history. A visitors' center adjoined, with superb photographs of her sailings. Curious tourists climbed to her pilothouse, gazing down toward Duchess, the pert little railway engine of Taku Town and Scotia Bay fame. A little further beyond stood Matthew Watson's General Store, still operating today. It had provided groceries and supplies to thousands of would-be gold miners. Nearby one could see the pioneer Carcross Hotel, out front a horse-drawn jitney sleigh which once carried winter passengers food and freight before days of the railway.

In her heyday, *Tutshi* was the talk of the North. Her journey was a unique excursion. Passengers who left the train and boarded her could well be described as the well-to-do. These remarkable folk regard themselves as professional travelers. Accustomed to a preferred standard wherever whim took them, they insisted on formally dressing for dinner. Below on the freight deck stood their steamer trunks, containing stylish gowns for the ladies, tux and velvet smoking jackets for the men. Often accoutrements included beakers of private ale, special blends of baccy and pipe racks. I was handed a ring of keys at Carcross as they boarded and kept up a steady traffic between cabins and trunks.

During the trip, the ladies paraded about in current fashions, often heard bewailing their fate to be in a untamed wilderness where decent millinery was hardly possible in what they called treacherous winds. These folks had wintered in warm, exotic climes such as the French Riviera, Caribbean, South Seas and the Vale of Kashmir. They had seen and done it all. Now they strolled about, men's pipes a-puff, their mates chittering away while some of the world's most magnificent scenery passed unappreciated on either side.

Sometimes, as the season waned, this type of folk were not so thick. In Whitehorse, a one-time waiter on *Tutshi*, Lawry Cyr, once told me of an incident on the ship. Three rather voluminous ladies presented themselves to him at Carcross. Two were to be in one cabin, the other elsewhere. One lady was very stout. She announced a preference for the upper bunk. Cyr took one look and fetched a short ladder from the freight deck. With help from her mate and heavy heavings from the steward, the big one was at last hoisted aloft. She lay there, well wedged. I asked Cyr what happened then. "I dunno," said he. "I took the ladder back down and steered clear of that cabin."

No matter what caliber of visitor, word had reached them about a clutch of waters far to the Canadian north, known as the Southern Lakes of Yukon. One could scan a travel folder, picturing a narrow-gauge railway crossing a snowy White Pass. It was possible to sit in sheltered armchair warmth and look down on snowy trails where thousands of gold-crazed men had toiled. Far below were signs poking up through the white, like Dead Horse Gulch, where horses by the score had perished.

But it was not the journey that drew these rich and not-so-rich travelers. They had heard of a far-off "oasis of international peace," which lay at the head of a wilderness lake, where an hospitable couple actually lived year-round, mid acres of huge flowers and vegetables. World leaders such as President Teddy Roosevelt, Britain's Prince of Wales, Canada's Governor General Lord Byng of Vimy, had inscribed their names there in a visitors book, left cards in appreciation. Such a place simply had to be seen if one was to keep in society's swim, or be one jump ahead of neighbors or fellow businessmen.

Now they were aboard *Tutshi*, soon to enter Nares Narrows, cross the mouth of Windy Arm, on Tagish Lake. At Ten Mile Point, often a boat put out because the lake was shallow. Norma Yardley and her father Gordon came alongside in a small boat and threw

150-200 pound burlap sacks of freshly caught lake trout on board. Passengers described them as delicious. After the joys of Ben-My-Chree travelers returned to Carcross in quiet mood, their minds filled with memories of an exceptional couple, cultured, genuinely hospitable, the kind who were a treasure to know as continuing friends.

For me, at season's end, it was back to *Aksala*, moored in a slough at Stewart City. Another deckhand and I were left aboard to bed down the ship. That meant stripping all linen and mattresses, table linen, kitchen gear and draining a hundred pipes. Al was a pleasant, easy-going chap, anxious to attend to things mechanical. All went well. We had two days before pickup. We decided to make a batch of ice-cream. Like most men, we stepped up sugar and canned cream, cranked away with gusto and before long had a gourmet delight. In fact, it was so rich Al took to the ship's side. I didn't feel so good myself. Then the upriver steamer blew and we were off to Whitehorse and Outside. Little did I know where that season on Yukon's sternwheelers would lead nor what adventures would unfold.

Back in Victoria, I sought out a local branch of the Bank of Montreal. I had several uncashed checks from White Pass to deposit. I had no need of much money up North, did not smoke or booze, and so never cashed my checks. It seemed reasonable to open an account from which I could purchase a long-cherished motorcycle. The teller refused to accommodate me. So did the accountant. The manager, into whose lofty office a properly indignant young man was ushered, pointed out dispassionately that I had no driver's license, no credit reference, nothing to prove who I was and no permanent address. Upon hearing of this affair, my adopted father donned his clergyman's collar (he affectionately called it his dog collar) and journeyed in from Mayne Island on the next ferry. Drawing himself up in a style reserved for recalcitrant members of his flock, he identified the Great Northern Adventurer. Only then would those stodgy bankers deign to accept my hard-earned dollars. The years passed and I again dealt with Montreal's bank in Vancouver. This time I wanted money from them. I should have remembered that first encounter. In spite of strenuous public relations programs, they had improved little.

Chapter 2

Seven North

In 1966 at home were Pat and three of our children, an Alsatian called Tsawwassen and a chocolate-point Siamese boy-cat who we had named Tha Him after a Thailand village. One daughter had left the nest, so the live bodies totaled seven, a good round figure. It was impossible to know why, but I began to think of the North. I had met Pat before WWII in Victoria, we corresponded back and forth across the sea and we later married in Christ Church Cathedral. She became a willing adventurer who easily participated in many enterprises.

In my little three-room office, high in the old Birk's building in Vancouver, things were not going well. I had been publishing a monthly trade journal, *Tourism, Journal of the Visitor Industry*. It was popular, but the task of finding and keeping commission salesmen to sell advertising was all but hopeless. They came, they drank, they went. Capital was short, printing bills rising alarmingly.

I pulled a pad across the desk and scribbled the words Seven North. Good thought! Toss this whole publishing mess into the wastebasket and head North. How? Little money, a tiny car, certainly not fit or of a size to tackle the Alaska Highway. Finally, no job. We needed at least a truck, and a good one. I had always liked Fords. Back in Duncan days when managing a distributing dairy, my route foreman, Jim Thibodeau, had sold me on Ford trucks. We eventually had a dozen or so one-tons on the go. They were far and away the most dependable and durable on the market in those days. They faithfully made three hundred or more stops and starts seven days a week, hauling milk, cream, frozen foods, newspapers, greeting cards and more throughout Cowichan's valley. They braved rock-rimmed potholes on the infamous Cowichan Lake Road, tackled logging roads back of Shawnigan Lake, trans-shipped ten-gallon cans of milk to rail speeders bound for Port Renfrew, Nitinat and beyond. They always started, even on slushy, cold winter mornings at 3:00 A.M. And they outlasted our early mongrel fleet of Fargo, International, Chevrolet and Jeep.

A copy of *Fortune* magazine lay open on my desk. Displayed was an ad for the first pick-up truck designed to accept a small, self-contained entity called a camper. It was just hitting the market as competition to travel trailers. The new recreational idea was a Ford.

I grabbed the phone, dialed the B.C. truck division of Ford and told an astonished representative my family was about to launch "Seven North": a Shepherd dog, Siamese cat, three children, a man and his wife who would all travel up the Alaska Highway, through Yukon and Alaska, returning via White Pass & Yukon Route Railway to Skagway and down the coast by Alaskan and newly inaugurated British Columbia Ferry.

Whether or not the idea sparked that executive, or whether he was simply carried along by the desperate enthusiasm in my voice, we will probably never know, but he readily agreed to provide the first camper special available from a Vancouver dealer.

We were off! A hefty kick at the snowball poised on my mental hillside convinced fledgling Vanguard Campers of Richmond to lend a camper, followed in rapid succession by a Standard Oil courtesy credit card, Honda trail bike and generator, plus a host of other sponsors. A friendly sign-painter found himself caught up in the affair and within a week we strung his banner on the rig and headed North.

It was a grand adventure. The camper was not very large by today's standards, but somehow we managed to sort out cat from dog, children from adults, clean from dirty socks, film from dust. We kept a journal since our sponsors wished us to publish the journey in various house organs. I thought perhaps the yarn might revive my own *Tourism*. It was a good story, but *Tourism* was not savable.

We stopped often, unlimbered the cameras, admired superb scenery and wondered what the famous military road up ahead would be like. We had heard rumors of dust, dirt and worse, but the Federal Tourist Bureau in Ottawa denied all bad news, showering us with glossy folders depicting gorgeous girls lounging on glamorous lakeshores, huge fish, the Northern Lights and more.

We reached Dawson Creek, Mile Zero on the famous Alaska Highway, and dust. Oh that dust! As we barreled along the constantly winding, steeply banked dirt and gravel road, its terrors assailed us. Dust billowed up and enveloped us with the passing of every truck and automobile. Sometimes it was so thick and stifling we could see nothing, not even the radiator cap. We learned to slow down, pull off to the verge, and obey instructions from whoever manned the ditch seat, carefully tracking road edge until the cloud settled or was blown to roadside. Meanwhile the wretched stuff crept around doors, windows and through a multitude of tiny cracks in both truck and camper. Although we plastered paint tape everywhere, we swallowed a lot of dust. Nobody, especially Mother, was happy.

Another joy was mud. In those days, highway crews employed a unique method of smoothing out portions of the highway yet to be black topped. The system dampened dust which, when dry, formed a surface smooth and hard. Water was pumped from wayside streams and reservoirs into truck tankers and sprayed on the highway which was then graded to a two-foot ridge at road center. A bare half-auto lane was left on each side while more grading brought the pile back to road width. The result? A two-inch layer of muck, enriched with sodium sulphate which eventually hardened. Until the next rain, or overly heavy truck traffic, the slurry became an excellent surface, smoother than pavement, and much easier to repair.

During the wet stage, vehicles became real mudders. Everything and everybody was plastered with half an inch of mud which dried like mortar. The only hope of survival was to keep the windshield washer fluid topped up, several changes of clothes handy and hope for the best. Mud became a badge of honor as we progressed. It was easy to spot an Alaska Highwayer in towns and cities, sometimes all the way down to Vancouver. Probably the rig has been off on a side-trip such as the Dempster or Cassiar highways if you see one today. The Alaska Highway proper is now almost all blacktop. Alaska is fully paved. That's a little sad. Not only are the banked curves disappearing, attacked by hordes of make-work highway crews, but as traffic increases and the pavement presses on, wilderness and adventure long associated with this pioneer road disappears. An elderly hunter-hiker once told me, "Where you have a difficult mountain trail to a lake you find beauty, peace and fish. Then comes a four-wheel track and with it beer cans, cigar butts, little beauty, peace or fish. Run blacktop in there and pretty soon you can forget it all for there remains only wall-to-wall people."

We arrived in Whitehorse and discovered a bright entrepreneur. He had built a high-roofed drive-through wash shed for trucks and campers. He had installed several coin-operated jet spray machines with which an owner could wash the mud off his rig. Part of his time was spent shoveling layers of muck out of the wash building. Often his face bore a sizable grin as he collected cascades of quarters from his coin boxes into a leather pouch dangling from substantial haunches. Although I tried valiantly then, and in later years, to whip his system, I found it impossible to run through the operation under three dollars.

He had a pump down by the Yukon River in order to avoid city water costs, used no detergent or heat, and allowed that he managed to make "about fifty thou" in a three-month season. In his quiet period, after returning from a break in Hawaii, he ordered up several cases of orange-juice-size cans, slapped an attractive label around each after inserting two teaspoonfuls of gravel. The label described contents as "The Genuine Article, Pure Alaska Highway Dust." He sold them at one dollar a pop. He was one happy Yukoner.

On the highway we came to recognize the advantages of our camper special. We were high off the road and enjoyed the best of sightseeing. We could zip off into a gravel pit and camp, or crawl up a side road, to bed down alongside a little lake, drifting off to sleep with loons singing their mating song. It was an ideal rig, one we still use. Eventually, we even taught Ford to dust-proof their western trucks. "Have you driven a Ford-lately?" Yep.

Also in Whitehorse we visited Yukon's tourist bureau, gave an interview to *The Whitehorse Star*, whose masthead motto is quite famous: "*Illegitimae du Carborundum*," liberally interpreted by Yukoners as "Don't let the b*****ds grind you down!" Then we all sank into a delicious hot bath. Travel a la wash basin is passable for short periods, but real relief from that dust and mud lies only in the long soak.

On to Dawson we drove, taking a dip in Takhini Hot Springs a few miles out of Whitehorse. My much-loved old sternwheeler *Keno*, the very last of her kind to puff downriver from Whitehorse, is dry-moored beside the Yukon River at Dawson. The family trekked up her gangplank. Memories crowded into my mind. Noises and voices filled my ears as I stood on her wood deck alongside the boiler. There were the wood trucks of old rumbling down, there was sweat, swearing and dirt. Up aloft everlasting deck rails stretched forth, covered with funnel smut, awaiting my soapy rag. Underfoot on upper decks were waves of hot clinkers piled up once more against lifeboat stanchions like sullen black snow. Aft of a familiar engine room and galley was my cramped lower berth, with a paddle-wheel slapping noisy water, where a starboard piston had belched steam and bathed me constantly. Such was the life of a deckboy. I loved it.

We prowled the old capital's streets, photographed historic buildings, stood in the yard of Robert Service's cabin. Out on famous Klondike creeks we relived gold rush days. Then up rocky hillsides, marveling at the still-present shovels, picks, pieces of rusty stoves, remains of rusting cans; here and there a few tattered logs, all that remain of a rough cabin in which men had crouched beneath low ceilings, desperately sifting the results of back-breaking labor from rocker and sluice (a long, wooden trough in which gravel containing gold is washed). Deep in smoke-filled shafts they had toiled for months, tending little fires, thawing their way foot by foot through permafrost to bedrock, wheezing and coughing for dank hours, endless days. Some found their bonanzas. Most did not. They wound up slaving for other owners, eventually gave up and dragged themselves home, health and spirit gone.

We found one of the last working gold dredges. The huge mechanical monster puffed and ground along a stream bed, hauling itself into self-made pools, yarding gravel into a gaping maw, spewing it out behind in tailings. Somewhere in the clanking midst, the machine extracted whatever gold Klondike miners had missed. There was something obscene about that dredge. It seemed vulgar, grasping.

From the air nowadays all that remains of this golden valley are the tailings, ugly worm droppings as far as the eye can see. From the storied Dome above Dawson they forever mar a beauty which was once pristine Yukon. When last we saw the diggings in 1986, modern mine operators with massive bulldozers and sluice-boxes were still extracting gold from these tailings. It was the third time around.

The Porter entourage drove on over what is called The Skyline Trail, first having boarded a quaint little ferry on the Dawson side of Yukon River. We marveled at a never-to-be forgotten color experience. We stopped several times to view and photograph almost limitless panoramas of rolling hills, clad in a thousand autumnal shades of birch trees. On one of our stops, another traveler turned in behind us and out popped a bright American lady. "It looks just like someone threw an afghan rug over everything!" she cried. It was an apt description, one that I used in articles which followed.

We crossed into Alaska and arrived at Tok Junction. The gravel gave way to astonishing blacktop and we bowled along in silent luxury. "Look Dad!" shouted Stephanie. "There's a moose!" Right by the roadside it browsed away, now and then raising a massive head, not at all concerned with the growls of Tsawwassen, nor with an abundance of craned necks. She crossed the road, regally pausing politely to have her photograph taken. As shutters clicked, an Alaskan and his family drove up. The driver leapt out, rushed up to us and sternly cautioned against moose, this one in particular. He pointed out the huge, lumbering beasts were an excitable bunch, given to unpredictable behavior, and could be quite dangerous. We thanked him and retreated to our vehicle. Lady moose ambled off, treated us to a "we are not amused" look, and passed from sight. We listened as she made her way into the silence of an unbelievable screen of multicolored fall leaves.

41

We had barely mounted up and gone a way toward Fairbanks, when an amateurishly painted roadside sign brought us up, short and excited. "Husky pups for sale! Good sled dogs." This was a must, not only for the youngsters, but for Pat and I. We pulled into a rough driveway and made ourselves known to a charming and hospitable young hostess and her pioneer family.

As we sat chatting in their log home, an ever-increasing uproar began to penetrate our conversation. It seemed to be coming from out back, so we followed our smiling new friend and stood on a rear porch. As we watched, the noise grew louder, wilder. Suddenly, on the roughest of trails, there appeared a very large dog, blue eyes sparkling, long pink tongue dripping, panting, feet pounding up the dust. Right behind came another, then two more, until perhaps a dozen straining, barking, joyous canines appeared, teamed in leather harness to a stripped-down Volkswagen chassis. Feet firmly planted on this astonishing vehicle, red baseball cap askew, flourishing beard streaming over a shoulder, stood our host, shouting encouragement, cracking a long leather whip carefully over the racing huskies.

The hullabaloo was horrendous! Then they were gone, across a partly-cleared field and away off into the brush again, only to emerge minutes later, brought to a dust-filled lathering halt in front of a totally awed Porter audience.

Thus we met our first Alaskans. They were members of The Church of Jesus Christ of Latter Day Saints—the Mormons—famous for historic treks across America to the great Salt Lake basin in Utah. They had turned north from Salt Lake City and, like an early Mormon prophet, had proclaimed of their Alaskan homestead, "This is the place!"

These good and generous people filled us with local Alaskan lore and kindly directions. They piled our larder full of fresh vegetables, even a well-hung moose roast. And of course, we never forgot those four soft, round furry bundles of lick and wiggle and smear, the husky puppies. Their mother, a gentle, mixed-breed animal, allowed us unlimited freedom with her family, probably only too happy for a short respite from those demanding appetites and sharp little teeth. The visit was a highlight among many.

Eventually we reached Fairbanks, then Anchorage. There were innumerable historic and scenic side-trips in between. We toured astonishing gardens, where huge and tasty vegetables vied with the largest strawberries we have ever seen. Shortly therafter, we swung back to Whitehorse on an alternate route. We found yet another milestone in what was beginning to become what eldest son Kim aptly called The Porter Saga.

When first Seven North arrived in Yukon's capital, we had chatted with the territorial tourist chief who was not only struggling with an oversize task of promoting and controlling a burgeoning horde of visitors, but pinch-hitting as centennial commissioner, trying to breath life into a program of celebrations to commemorate Yukon's part in Canada's one hundredth birthday party. We had also met a newly appointed territorial commissioner, Jim Smith, and his assistant commissioner, Frank Fingland, who told us there was urgent need for a full-time coordinator to keep up their end in Expo '67.

Fingland had earlier viewed the Seven North gang, was apparently impressed, and inquired whether I would be interested in taking on the job for perhaps a year. We had agreed to think it over on the Alaskan leg. By now the family had debated itself almost out the camper door. We finally seized opportunity and adventure one more time. Stephanie quoted Shakespeare, settling with the sure wisdom of youth any qualms we oldsters might have had. Said she: "Dad, there comes a time and a tide in the affairs of men which, taken at the flood, leadeth on to fortune. I think you should take it!"

Well, that was some flood. By the time it subsided, we were well into the land development business, had established a fledgling real estate company and purchased a wilderness homestead at the head of Tagish Lake. The quest for Ben-My-Chree had begun. We borrowed the down payment!

We returned to Vancouver and set matters there in some sort of order. I flew north, a somewhat bewildered centennial commissioner, a one-man band whose task was to establish a series of events and projects of caliber and excitement appropriate to Yukon's place in Canada's one hundredth birthday. It was a great challenge. Already I loved the North and this wild territory's past, present and future. Now I was to travel to every nook and cranny of that mighty land, seek out her people and hope to translate their wishes into a boisterous and lasting historic celebration.

In Whitehorse I batched, chin-deep in centennial affairs. Fathoming federal, territorial and city files and government ways of doing business was an adventure in itself. There were to be celebrations at Whitehorse, Dawson, Watson Lake, Destruction Bay, Old Crow, Mayo, Elsa and so on. One young fellow wrote to say he would be raising a special flag-pole at his home on Tagish Lake. His name was Jim Brook. We would come to know him and his family in our quest for Ben-My-Chree.

What did we do? There was never a dull moment. We ran a Yukon flag competition, created the Yukon navy, and let contracts for community halls, cairns, and even a four-hole bathroom at Destruction Bay—insulated, running water, modern as all getout. There was a superb mountain climb by members of the Canadian Alpine Club, who named several peaks in the Kluane Lake area.

Then one day, while poring over old files, I stumbled on an abandoned project: the building of a Yukon centennial pavilion at Expo, Montreal. Previously the budget had been deemed too small, costs too high, and the whole idea had been shelved in a cloud of negativism. Yet such a project would return the investment a thousand-fold in visitors eager to see for themselves the land of the Klondike.

The time seemed ripe to paint bright word pictures. I suggested a log cabin of white birch logs in which would be displayed a number of gold bricks in a bullet-proof case. Moose, goat and bear heads would peer down from walls. Beautiful Yukon maidens, dressed in gold-rush costumes would act as hostesses, RCMP constables, clad in scarlet, shining boots and Stetson would guard the entrance.

The idea, like most good ones, invited criticism. It was, said the naysayers, ridiculous, outrageous, impractical, expensive, even dangerous. Because of all that uproar, it succeeded. The bright-eyed and bushy-tailed tribe, of which most communities have at least one, rose to the occasion. Flo Wyard, *Whitehorse Star* editor; Roy Minter, public relations officer White Pass & Yukon Route; and a host of willing organizations and citizens clasped the project to their bosoms, and began to shout. I flew to Montreal to find space which

I was advised did not exist. In a siege of the Expo commissioner, I showed him a massive moose head. When he saw that, he caved in, shoe-horning us into a prime space.

Back home, I rose in Yukon community meetings, told about a need for birch logs, furnishing and staffing. It was a good story. Besides, most of the RCMP detachments in Yukon wanted to see Expo! Press, radio and CBC television picked it up. I shamelessly played on Territorial pride, throwing in a dash of local politics. When faced with stony glares at the outset, I let fly a clarion cry.

"Are we going to let all these bureaucrats defeat a damn good idea?"

"No, we are not!" roared audiences from Elsa to Destruction Bay.

I was able to persuade Shirley Jensen, Yukon's tourist supervisor, to keep an eye on our hostess girls in Montreal, while they manned our pavilion. The day arrived when Commissioner Jim Smith opened Yukon's very own Expo "Gold Pavilion." Thousands of visitors saw the moose head, the gold and the girls, and tightened up plans to visit an historic territory. It had been just a little harder to accomplish the impossible.

There were some fun times during Expo. Not all projects worked out. Some were hilarious failures, some sad disappointments. It is hard to forget the beautification of Whitehorse project. One day a determined little man in jeans and sneakers strolled into my office and asked if I was Cy Porter. Then he slapped down a check for $25,000, with my name on it. I had no idea that this was Al Kluan, famous prospector and mining millionaire. Al told me he did not trust government, but had heard the centennial bloke was honest. I told him there was no way I could accept a personal check, even for so fine a program as planting trees along the streets of Whitehorse. We compromised by rounding up a committee comprised of Mayor Howie Firth; Dave Robertson, owner of the *Yukon News;* and myself to oversee spending that generous gift.

I wrote the universities of Alaska and Edmonton, the Arctic Institute and other organizations, rounding up various types of hardy shrubs and trees. We enlisted the city of Whitehorse workers to build tree and flower tubs, and water and maintain the flow of foliage. As fast as we got the trees planted, wild weekend partiers in from the mines on a Friday night, eager to destroy parking meters futilely installed by city fathers, drove purposely into tubs and trees. Other foliage graced various residential boulevards, where malamutes cocked potent legs and so cursed every flower and bush. Then came the frost, snow and freeze. By spring, nary a bush nor tree had survived. The committee elected to deposit what remained of the Kluan Fund into general centennial revenue, where I did my best to make it count. Al Kluan has gone now, like many of the centennial helpers, but I am sure Yukoners remember him and his kind wish.

Then there was the Perpetual Northern Light project which, unfortunately, I inherited. It was destined from the beginning not to even flicker. No matter how hard we strove, including the centennial committee, that copper pipe dream refused to gel. It was to have been a wavy, wandering creation, mounted in front of the post office and what was the old administration building in Whitehorse. The thought was to fire the light with propane. Many forces were allied against it from the beginning. Fire marshals rose up and with them insurance wallahs. Lawn lovers saw destruction to a precious green sward. Designers sketched and competed, but as fast as they brought forth, welders and blacksmiths cried out impractabilities. Finally, I gave in, gradually starved the affair of publicity, gently and a little sadly letting the file lie quietly in a distant cabinet where I have no doubt it rests to this day, unhallowed and certainly unlit.

Other projects swam lustily. Like the Yukon River Flotilla, which started out, at least in my mind, as a real sleeper. The idea that boating manufacturers and canoers, kayakers and the cream of all that floats would flock in from Outside to a turbulent river seemed rather far-fetched. After all, the whole of Canada was awash with exciting projects during this centennial year, and we were a trifle short of advertising funds. But we gave it a good whack. Letters and folders went out to marine engine firms, boat builders, canoe manufacturers, anything remotely concerned with water travel. Weeks went by. Nothing. Then a few replies trickled in. Derek Irons, president of the Yukon Fish and Game Club, had fits. It wouldn't fly.

Then the dam broke. He was overwhelmed by sacks of entries. All manner of craft, individual and commercial wanted in! Derek coped manfully. Dragooning the army, air force, RCMP into the fray, he solved logistics such as portable outhouses on river bars, food drops, safety concerns, law and order, booze control. The entries continued to grow; miraculously all went well, no accidents, no one was hurt, no one even got wet. All arrived at Dawson on time and, literally, full of beans and perhaps a snort or two.

The year came and went. I returned to Vancouver, pursued the land game, selling recreational and retirement beaches in the Gulf Islands and along the B.C. coast. We founded our own Pacific Shore Realty Ltd. Three years later, in 1971, thanks to a word from Roy Minter, White Pass & Yukon Route sold Ben-My-Chree to us. The whole quest seemed preordained.

Chapter 3

Discovery

Ben-My-Chree had its beginning when prospectors began to search the shores, valleys and mountains of Tagish Lake. With the establishment of Engineer Mine, comprised of a group of hard-rock claims, prospectors began to explore areas in the immediate vicinity. Many claims were recorded across the lake on the flanks of White Moose Mountain, Big Horn and similar rivers.

The first claim at lake head was posted by an employee of the mine named Stanley McLellan. From diaries and other records, here is his personal story.

He rested, paddle lying thankfully cross-gunwale, down a little by the blade—his shoulders tended that way also—accumulated shaft water flowing down naturally, seeking return to mother lake. The canoe gradually relinquished momentum, bow wave subsiding to a ripple, to nothing.

Just behind his silent canoe lay a sharp peninsula. Trees—pines, always pines—marched amidst rough rock, narrowing their line to a sharp point, like a Roman phalanx, until at last only one, a sentinel, faced the lake. One day, in remembrance of a British headland, the point would be named Holyhead, yet another attempt by lonely wanderers to civilize this wild land. The taming would never wholly succeed.

He felt a surge of security, relief to find the tiny baylet, a brief opportunity to shelter from short, uneven waves just out beyond the bay's perimeter. He thought of them as whitecaps, feared and respected by turn. Sailors, men who go down to the sea in ships, that do business in great waters sometimes called them white horses, angry heaps, albino manes urged into frantic gallop by a master wind seemingly intent on battle against some mystical castle.

Stanley McLellan's nature seldom permitted his lean muscular body to relax. Rarely did he pause to contemplate a varied life to where he was now, an experienced prospector. His face, permanently pale where unkempt salt-and-pepper beard protected deeply lined features, gave way to a rugged tan. His skin had weathered strong winds, blizzards, exposure to valley and mountain sun. His eyes were pale blue, bleached by glare from a land they constantly searched.

He was accustomed to the North's moods, like poker hands, to be played with skill, a little bluff, losing most of the time, but now and then savoring amidst the smoke of life the unusual joy of winning. Today he held a promising hand. He harbored a precious secret—gold!

A little way up a granite wall high in the mountains sheltering a river-laced delta at the lake's southern end, he had found something which caused his doubting heart to leap, normally deliberate paces to swiften. There, half again his height, part of white speckled granite, was a dull yellowish vein. It disappeared all too soon, but he clawed a way up, excitement powering his prospector's pick, he chipped away, each inch fueling another stroke. The vein vanished, and then appeared again.

Gold is found in lode deposits, like McLellan's, in hard rock. Lode deposits, the original source of placer gold, are mineral deposits found within fissures of rock. Prospectors who discovered this type usually lease or sell their mining rights to sizable mining groups or companies with sufficient equipment and capital to develop the find. Most gold, like that discovered in Klondike and Atlin, is of a variety called placer. These deposits are found in streams and river beds as grains and nuggets By water, wind and erosion they are washed from the lode and carried downstream. Other sources appear as a minor element in porphyry copper and in sea water. By far the greatest untapped world reserves of gold lie in the oceans where untold tons are dissolved.

Only a tiny percentage of gold in our planet's crust has been found up to now; something like .0002 of 1 percent. So there is hope for the prospector yet.

McLellan hastened down to timber line, chopped several pine posts, shaped a point at one end and squared about six inches at the other. Then up again, taking direction by compass, pacing out a legal claim, marking the post, striving to map what might very well become a lifetime's dream fulfilled—gold!

Weary, he squatted down on a sloping surface. A ptarmigan clucked in bushes below. The bird came into sight, camouflaged in summer plumage, brown, gray, with flecks of white. McLellan swiftly reached for his .22 rifle. One shot, a small fire made a hunter's supper, then down to Tagish shores, seeking out a hidden canoe, embarking. For a few miles a rocky east shore was his guide, paddling in green silted waters. The lake took its shade from a glacial river, its source far up-valley where ice fields slowly melted.

The canoe lay lightly. His possessions were minimal: worn pack, short-handled ax, prospector's pick, rifle, a small bag of dry beans, and some salt and sugar measured only in teaspoons. But there was a tiny moose-hide bag tied tightly with a leather thong. It contained chips of granite in which shone veins of softly glistening metal. Prospectors are not given much to conversation, but now he muttered over and over: "Gold."

He realized an immediate task was to register the claim with the government's Department of Mines through a northern agent, either in Atlin or Carcross. He sought companionship too. Engineer Mine, a sizable gold operation, lay some ten miles down lake. Surprisingly, this desire for fellowship, to share a gold find, was primary, a tradition long cherished among prospectors. So strong was the need to share, that government mining regulations of the day stipulated any person discovering gold was entitled to stake a discovery claim and another claim downstream known as Number One Below. Other miners were free to stake numerically above and below these claims on hearing of the find.

Thus in wanting to share his find, McLellan followed the typical prospector's behavior pattern: to be somewhat mysterious, to boast a little and display gold samples which caused eyes to light up, fever start to rise. Friends would learn where the claim was located. This was common treasure among those who searched the land, ostensibly seeking tangible wealth, but in reality rewarded more by searching than actual discovery.

McLellan's sinewed arms drove his paddle tip forward and down, strongly sternward in the automatic rhythm favored by those whose life married lake with mountain. The canoe began to quarter small waves near shore. He smiled and dipped his paddle deeper, increasing stroke. There were miners at Engineer, the promise of good talk, a warm cookhouse and plenty of food, laughter and understanding. Reginald Brook Sr., partner and mine manager at Engineer, was a good friend. So was Captain James Alexander, principal owner. Engineer produced gold certainly, but costs of drilling, driving tunnels, payroll, supplies and freight left little room for profit. Production was spasmodic, in part due to constant frustration in tracing underground veins of varying quality, and the coming and going of transient miners, an uncertain breed who often signed on out of desperation. They had failed to find fortune along the creeks of Atlin, the Klondike and a hundred river bars. They might have passed beyond Dawson to Nome, Alaska, searching tidal beaches there, ever searching, seeking fortune until at last they ran out of food and courage, fearing above all a return to distant home where less adventurous neighbors, even loved ones, might scorn and condemn.

After a few days at Engineer, McLellan bid farewell to his sourdough brothers, shoved off and began the long paddle to Carcross, where Tagish, Nares and Bennett Lakes mingled their waters. A number of pioneer settlers along Tagish shores would provide shelter and welcome. Visitors were rare; not only was it an honored Yukon custom to feed and bed down a traveler, the chance of a yarn with another human was not be to missed.

No smoke was coming from Brook's place, a cabin just east of Golden Gate, a few miles beyond Engineer. One of the first surveyed blocks of land on what was known as the Southern Lakes, Brooklands, at the mouth of Rupert Creek, was recognized as a friendly way-point where the main body of Tagish extended Graham Arm toward Taku Town. Near by was a box, shaped like a wee house, hung in a tree at a point by the water's edge. It was a mail box, where prospectors, miners and settlers received and sent their mail. It is still there today.

In earlier days there had been a trail from Engineer to Brooklands, from where it led to Taku Town, and the two miles of trail-cum-wagon road paralleling the short and swift Atlin River. It was all part of the original water and land route familiar to Indians, explorers and gold seekers in their linkage of ocean with inland lakes and rivers. The tiny riverside wagon road would become one of the world's shortest railways.

He shaped course to a sheltered bay beyond Deep Bay. One day it would be named after a moorage known in Jamaica: Port Royale. Next day saw him approaching Potter's Point, then Tutshi, Squaw Point and Ten Mile Point. Countless paddle strokes ruffled the lake, until at last he passed the mouth of Windy Arm into Nares Lake and River, and came in sight of the clapboard Carcross Hotel.

He treated himself to the luxury of a hot bath with real bed to follow. Learning of his search for a grubstake, others told him of a man named Otto Partridge who managed a sawmill at Millhaven Bay, some eight miles off West Bay on Lake Bennett. Partridge was said to have a dollar and be an adventuresome sort.

Next morning McLellan set out for Millhaven. He was made welcome. Otto and Kate Partridge, Emily Dalton and Ludwig Swanson listened to the report of his claim and carefully examined the ore samples. All were impressed. Partridge agreed to provide food for the prospector. In a day or so supplies were rounded up and the two set forth in the sailing sloop, towing McLellan's canoe. The hope that a mine would come about was strong. Gold!

Chapter 4

The Tides of Life

The founder of Ben-My-Chree, Otto Hawker Partridge, was born in England's Hertfordshire County in 1855. His parents took him and his younger brother to the Isle of Man, enrolling them at King William's, a famous school located a mile or so from Castletown on the Isle's southern tip. Like many a King William's boy, Otto liked to hike the two miles to Douglas and look out over the harbor. Deep-sea steamers wallowed their way through North Channel, round the Calf of Man, inbound to Liverpool, or out onto the Atlantic, shaping course for the New World.

Names such as America, Canada, Mexico and Northwest Passage stirred Partridge's imagination. Harbor smells and ocean tang must have spun a magic web, and in Manx tradition, by fourteen years of age he apprenticed to the Mercantile marine. At nineteen, with his brother, he sailed for San Francisco, California, intending to link up with an older brother, perhaps to take advantage of ships bound for ports even further afield.

When the two arrived, they were told their brother had gone to New Orleans, address unknown. The United States and Mexico were in a state of near war at the time and, lacking immediate employment, they enlisted in the U.S. Navy for three years, obtaining special dispensation from Washington, since they were not yet nationalized Americans.

Tour of duty over, in 1880 Otto returned to England to claim a sizable legacy. He courted and married Fanny Kate, a cousin he had long admired and corresponded with since age nine. She was a quiet young English gentlewoman, well-mannered, able to preside with dignity and aplomb over traditional afternoon tea in the approved two lumps, cream or lemon style.

One wonders if this closeted young lady would have been dismayed had she known the part she would play in Klondike's saga. It is unlikely she imagined a life of hunting, fishing, climbing mountains, sailing lakes and rivers in a pristine wilderness far from kith and kin in a land where the presence of a woman was in itself unique.

Otto had pursued other fair maidens in the course of his travels. One such, Polly Tarbox, in 1928, turns up in some of his letters toward the end of his life at Ben-My-Chree.

Partridge took his bride overseas to California where earlier he had come to know warm and pleasant agricultural areas in the expanding American West. He described their adventures in the same letters above:

> Went to fruit ranching in a large way and succeeded well until the bottom dropped out of the fruit market and we had to sell our peaches to the canneries at $6 a ton, whilst it cost us $7 a ton for picking alone.

They made the best of it. Before them stretched unbroken waves of spring fruit blossoms in the Santa Clara valley. It was scenes like this which charmed them both, setting in motion a lifelong interest in horticulture.

On July 15th, 1897, a ship named *Excelsior* sailed into San Francisco harbor from the far North bearing, as a local newspaper claimed, "a ton of gold." In no time at all the whole continent was on fire with the word Klondike, a wild northern territory where local headlines told of fortunes waiting to be scooped up in the form of gold nuggets plainly visible in stream beds. Miners continued to stagger down West Coast gangplanks, barely able to carry bulging suitcases, kit bags, blankets and rough wooden boxes filled with gold found in places like British Columbia, Yukon and Alaska. Captains faced the almost impossible task of holding crews to handle ships bound for anywhere other than the North. Sailors jumped ship whenever opportunity afforded, signing on to anything headed for Klondike.

A friend wrote Otto from Victoria, British Columbia, pleading with him to form a partnership into the wilds where, he said, gold could be found almost anywhere. Partridge carries on in his correspondence with Polly Tarbox:

> ...when the Klondike rush set in we quit farming and started forth for the north. Left my plucky little wife in Victoria, B.C., and came North with a Navigation Company in the capacity of a laborer at $3 per day. Four months later was made manager at $500 a month which they dated back to date of my joining the Company.

In spite of gold fever, Partridge was both prudent and entrepreneurial. By studying the best maps available, he saw an abundance of lakes and rivers lying between the northern Pacific Coast and lakes and rivers in Yukon Territory where gold was said to abound. Boats, perhaps even steamers, would be in demand. He had picked up a working knowledge of ship-building during Isle of Man days. With a stake of $20,000 stowed in a bale of caulking oakum, he was able to avoid the much feared Soapy Smith, whose gang ruled and robbed many passing through the towns of Skagway and Dyea, Alaska, jumping-off spots for passes leading to the gold fields further inland.

In those feverish, rumor-rife months, almost every coastal city in Canada and the United States turned out booklets and maps, attempting to lure the ignorant and unaware to unscrupulous merchants eager to charge whatever the trade would bear for shoddy equipment, poor food. Many a Klondike pilgrim found himself and his sorry gear landed at a tiny, little-known hamlet on the north coast, rimmed by mountains and glacial ice—uncharted and forbidding. Some struggled along fairytale trails to continental interiors, braving river rapids, falls, swamps and mountain bluffs which crushed eager spirits, stilled brave hearts and turned minds inward toward insanity.

Partridge and his partner hiked over the infamous Chilkoot Pass, sharing hardship with hordes of frantic good seekers. They struggled in lockstep up a hazardous snow and ice trail, hiring Indian packers to transport the required ton of goods per man demanded by Canadian Northwest Mounted Police who held the summit. Ironically, their stubborn presence ensured not only safety for the prospectors, but laid claim to what would become the future boundary between Alaska, British Columbia and Yukon. The mountie outpost enabled a future international boundary commission to recognize possession as prime support for Canada's claim to much of this wild country.

When the two partners arrived at last on the shores of Lake Bennett, they stood amazed at the scene. Bennett's shores contained a sea of tents; they crowded the streams and lake shore, reaching into the hills above, where stood row upon row of stumps, witness to the demand for logs. These would be whipsawed into green planks, used to build all manner of watercraft. Everywhere hundreds of men toiled to build vessels, flat-bottomed simple boats, barges, rafts, in which they hoped to somehow traverse the 560 miles of lake and river to Dawson, by sail, oar or paddle. Between the tents lay stacks of firewood, used to keep warm and cook amidst bitter cold.

The greatest challenge of boat-building was whipsawing logs into planks. In the rush to create lumber, one man stood atop a platform onto which a log had been rolled. His partner, in a pit below, held a long double-handled saw linking the two. Up and down went the blade, cutting only on the down swing. The man below found himself showered by face-burning pitchy sawdust. On top of that, his buddy "up there" was certainly slacking, slow and uncertain on the up-stroke. Within minutes each man had decided the other was not pulling his weight. So intense was their gold-fired ambition, so hostile and soul-searing this cruel labor, outbursts of wrath were inevitable. The upper man claimed his sawdust-enshrouded pal was the epitome of feebleness, while he believed himself to be both pushing and pulling far in excess of the easy job below.

Some pairs became so incensed they abandoned a lifetime friendship, dividing food and equipment on the spot, severing partnerships to the point where sacks of flour were cut in half, stoves smashed to pieces in the name of fair division. More than one ugly wooden skiff, almost completed, was sawn in half, so eager were partners to destroy a human relationship.

Partridge and his friend set to work as part of a group named Bennett Lake & Klondike Navigation Company. A shipyard and sheds rose on Lake Bennett's shores. Shares were sold to employees. Keels were laid for the Southern Lake's first sternwheel steamers, intended to serve Bennett, Tagish, Canyon City near Whitehorse and Atlin's goldfields. Steam boilers and machinery were ordered from Outside. Soon *Ora* then *Nora*, each some sixty feet in length, stood broadside by the lakeshore on greased timbers, waiting for the ice to melt. *Flora* would follow.

Passengers on these *"bateaux mouches"* were required to supply their own food and bedding on what was known as the bare bones fleet. One wag claimed the craft boasted fresh running water—bring your own pail and rope. Accommodation meant find whatever deck space was available and stretch out.

The small steamers played an important part in hauling freight, prospectors, girls and grandees from Bennett City to Dawson. In time they shot the treacherous Miles Canyon and Whitehorse rapids. Once through, it was difficult to return upstream to the lakes.

At Canyon City, another detachment of mounties monitored the hordes of boats, allocating a number to each, classifying owners as capable of traversing the dangerous waters ahead, or not. Women and children were removed, joining the unqualified on a wooden-tracked tramway, bypassing a part of the Yukon River which claimed many lives.

After waiting in Victoria for nearly a year, Kate Partridge went into the country hiking the same treacherous Chilkoot trail as her husband, helped along by gold seekers who were delighted to lend a hand to a real woman, one of the few whose presence brightened their harsh trail. It is rare to find photographs of women in the midst of the Chilkoot, for few of the fair sex were willing or able to face privation, snow, ice and blizzards.

An astonishingly complete photographic record of this saga has been left to us. Detail and clarity of pictures, often taken under the most trying conditions, are of high calibre. One such photographer, E. A. Hegg, had closed his two studios in Bellingham Bay, Washington. He assembled a portable darkroom and attached it to a sled drawn by four goats. He adapted normal studio procedures to the perils and weather of the North. It was necessary to heat his developer to keep it from freezing, filter water through charcoal and to coat wet plates with a mixture improvised from herbs and egg albumen. Heavy and sizable cameras had to be handled in forty-below temperatures. Yet in spite of these obstacles, Hegg's photographs of the gold rush on Chilkoot Pass and beyond were of surprising quality.

Kate Partridge and her companion were caught up in an adventure as ancient as the very unfolding of mankind—the search for a soft, glowing metal, valuable because of scarcity, difficult to discover and requiring immense labor to extract. Gold possessed the virtue of endurance, and with it a glowing wonderment which strangely attracted men. Beyond empires as great and greater than Egypt, gold had ever spawned a multitude of evils in the midst of humans. Genesis in the Bible tells us:

> A river went out of Eden to water the garden; and from thence it was parted, and became into four heads. The name of the first is Pison; that is it which compasseth the whole land of Havilah, where there is gold. And the gold of that land is good.

As in lesser world searches for this elusive metal, the strongest force flowing through the hordes comprising Klondike's goldrush, was man's inherent greed—an overwhelming desire to possess something rare and therefore valuable in the eyes of world societies. Yet in spite of this feverish determination, which at times bordered on madness, the vast majority of seekers on reaching Klondike's Dawson, ignored the goldfields, strangely content to walk up and down streets knee-deep in mud, ogling fabulously rich bonanza kings as they strolled in and out of hotel bars, a dance girl or lady of the night on each arm.

It is worthwhile to ponder for what had this host of desperate humanity left all civilized comfort, sold all worldly goods, cleaned out bank accounts, abandoned loved ones and friends? Was it to clutch gold in hands frostbitten and trembling, the badge of so-called security setting them apart from those left behind? If that be so, the mystery deepens, for by the time they reached the gold fields, having suffered physical and mental pain beyond reason, most sources of riches had long ago been claimed, nuggets and dust scraped from a thousand hills and stream beds. A strange determined few, still heeding a persistent call, pressed on to the beaches of Nome, Alaska, upon hearing rumors of yet another strike. Most arrived too late, the treasure found exhumed, gone Outside in the hands of more experienced, swifter sourdoughs.

Today, close to a hundred years later, we must conclude this massive adventure joined by Kate and Otto Partridge, was for most a journey to seek out the gold, not necessarily to find it. The seekers had reached their goal; it was enough; ever after their heads would be held high. They were winners with no prize other than overcoming monstrous obstacles and arriving.

When Kate finally reached Bennett City and fondly embraced her husband, she found him a buoyant part of this famous launching shore on the water route to both Atlin and Dawson's treasure. As managing director of a ship-building company, he and his little band of partners, shipwrights and laborers were busily engaged in building the first small sternwheel steamers. Supplies and gear for ships and barges were flowing in from Outside up the coast to Skagway. Somewhat crude but practical steam-powered hoists and gravity haulways now paralleled toiling Klondikers as the massive invasion of men, food and equipment moved over Chilkoot pass. On these cableways freight passed beyond Chilkoot's summit by sled and portaged over a succession of streams and lakes, mainly downhill, to Bennett. As 1897 faded and the key year, 1898, dawned, there seemed to be an almost imperceptible slackening of numbers. Word of frightening hazards, ice-bound mountains, almost impossible hardships requiring the physique of supermen, was beginning to filter back to civilization, carried by returning adventurers, some defeated, others ill.

At the same time, a courageous group of British investors, spurred on by visionary reports from early-day pioneers, such as Captain William Moore and George Brackett, were fashioning a dream from the reality of docks and wagon roads to creation of a narrow-gauge railway over a neighboring longer, but less steep mountain pass into Yukon's interior. That gateway was White Pass, long held as an impossibility through which to construct a railway; but once more, as with foot conquest of the Chilkoot, dreams combined with ambition as a spark to human determination. One of the world's fiercest construction feats was to become a profitable fact.

Kate Partridge was an assiduous chronicler of daily events. She kept a detailed diary from 1898, when Bennett became home, right up to shortly before her husband's death. Her diary begins in a tent on a Bennett sidehill. Later she moved into town, residing in the Thorpes Hotel, which doubled as a hospital. She had by now faced into harsh Yukon weather, beginning with winter rains, sleety snow and then blizzards. Temperatures dropped to fifty-four below zero one morning. By 11:00 A.M. it still stood at forty-five below. She tells of a Londoner who was brought in with both feet frozen, having struggled through snow and over ice from Atlin.

During these days she notes many comings and goings of stern-wheelers and hand-built boats. There was much movement of people, staking of mining claims around Bennett. Kate obtained her own mining license, fee $5. A lumber mill operated across the lake where steamers were pulled out during freeze-up. While lumber for steamer construction doubtless originated here, when town buildings required increased production, the timber sources began to wither.

Steamers carried people, mail and freight between Bennett, Carcross, Tagish and to the head of Miles Canyon. Another route was down Tagish Lake to Taku Town and so to Atlin.

Kate conducted a voluminous correspondence with her mother, relatives and a growing list of wives traveling with their husbands. The spirit of the day promoted liberal hospitality, followed quite soon by correspondence which transformed brief visits into lifelong friendships.

Aware that history was all about her, Kate purchased a Kodak outfit including developing and printing equipment. She photographed events down the years, but sadly this priceless record remains undiscovered. In addition to the three steamers built by Otto's company, a number of larger sternwheelers made their appearance, among them *Clifford Sifton*, *Ogilvie*, *Bailey*, *Kilbourne*, *Tasmanian* and *Gleaner*, most built in Bennett.

On November 21st, 1898, telephone wires were completed to Bennett, and while awaiting arrival of the new railway, the community felt bold enough to assume a touch of importance by adopting the larger name of Bennett City.

An interesting name crops up in Kate's diary about this time, that of Count Charbonneau. This surely is the same doubtfully titled person referred to in various Klondike chronicles as he who, on reaching Dawson, wooed and won Belinda Mulroney, famous goldrush businesswoman, entrepreneur and owner of the Grand Forks Fairview Hotel, close to the goldfields. Pierre Berton's *Klondike*:

> Belinda undoubtedly was the best catch in the Klondike for an enterprising bachelor. Such a man duly arrived on the scene. He sported a monocle, kid gloves, spats, and a small jet-black mustache, and a tall, bearded valet.

Into the Partridge's lives during these days came three people, each a strong character. During their Yukon years they would contribute in a remarkable way to the history of Ben-My-Chree and those who lived there. First upon the horizon was an English nobleman, Lord Maurice Edgerton. He possessed an international business reputation, and was an experienced big game hunter, always anxious to add to an already impressive trophy room. With him he brought a number of meticulously maintained guns calibred to down elephant, lion, tiger or ibex, as well as available water or land-based fowl. A collection of Hardy India split-cane fly rods with matching reels, each in its own immaculate velvet-lined case with tiny wrench and oil dropper, set him apart not only as a well-to-do sportsman, but one whose desire for excellence was matched by equipment.

By virtue of a seat in the British House of Lords, Edgerton had rubbed shoulders with fellow hunters of renown who traveled with him in search of game in various climes. He was well-funded and as a shrewd businessmen knew English financiers such as William Brooks Close, Close Brothers & Company, London, principals in the rapidly advancing White Pass & Yukon Railway. Close had met Otto Partridge and marked him as an adventurous and somewhat daring northern mover and shaker. Edgerton learned from Close that Partridge often took to the hills in search of wild meat, at the same time enjoying the hunt and fair chase.

Having written ahead, Edgerton sought out the Partridges. He was made welcome. Otto led him along river valleys and up mountains by Bennett Lake. Wilderness trails revealed abundant game. The two became warm friends within a few days as do Yukon hunters to this day. That friendship was to last a lifetime.

Kate Partridge, among other characteristics, was a devoted member of the Church of England. Not long after her arrival in Bennett City she organized a hymn sing, meeting Sundays in a tent. Later she lent her support to a group of Presbyterians raising funds from businessmen and Klondikers for construction of a lakeside church. The rough timber structure with spire and cross remains unfinished to this day, standing atop a hill, marker to those who strove to carry spiritual and moral standards into a wild land.

Bennett City, a once booming Klondike tent community, seemed destined to fade. No longer did hordes of gold-crazed pilgrims struggle over the Chilkoot, press on downhill over Crater, Long, Deep and Lindeman Lakes to the shores of Bennett. Otto, sensing a new era with reality of the White Pass & Yukon Railway, was ready to move on, leaving a floating legacy in the form of south Yukon's first sternwheeler steamers.

Partridge was accustomed to looking ahead to distant horizons. He now recognized the railway had a need for ties, trestle beams and bridge planks. He took Kate down to a small, heavily forested bay on Bennett's West Arm, not far from Carcross. They named the place Millhaven, in anticipation of establishing a rough lumber mill. Machinery was ordered Outside, shipped to Skagway and transported by railway flatcar to Watson, a new station almost opposite across the lake from Millhaven. Up and running in record time, the operation obtained a contract from the railway and soon became profitable. There was a demand for housing and commercial materials. Agencies were opened in Whitehorse and beyond.

The family occupied quarters in tents ashore at first, but later an old barge was towed down from Bennett. It was converted to a houseboat, with snug rooms afloat. Otto, Kate and Swanson, their long-time friend and handyman, soon took up residence. Kate presided over a kitchen with wood-fired cook stove. Kerosene lamps provided light, ice cut during winter months and stored for summer in an outhouse, provided refrigeration.

She soon had a hymn sing underway, first in a tent ashore, later on the houseboat. Everyone was encouraged to attend, including millhands. She made the acquaintance of William Carpenter Bompass, a Church of England Bishop, who had come to Carcross with his wife. Bompass, a member of a particularly valiant little band of religious pathfinders in the 1850s, was in the habit of striking out into the wilderness in an attempt to match efforts of Roman Catholic counterparts in capturing Indian and Eskimo souls in the far North. Although the good bishop impressed and spurred her Christian efforts, it was not he but a lady companion-housekeeper, provided by the Church Missionary Society in England, who would bring joy and substance to the Partridge menage. Her name was Emily Dalton. She had been originally recruited to keep Charlotte, the Bishop's wife, company while His Lordship charged off on far quests for months at a time. However, when Dalton arrived, she visited her school-day friend Kate at Millhaven, and promptly changed course, electing to become part of what she perceived as a much more exciting life. Kate welcomed the idea and soon Miss Emily was ensconced on the barge. The two explored lakeshore and mountains, setting fish nets and gathering wild berries which they transformed into jams and jellies.

With Otto, Emily trudged up through mountain valleys, learning to shoot, quarter and skin young goat, moose, caribou and handle a fowling piece for feathered booty. She was a staunchly built woman, rather formidable on first sight, but was not long in establishing a presence which was to prove invaluable in the Partridge's lives.

In response to a request for transportation to Carcross, Closeleigh, Whitehorse and Atlin, Otto built his beloved Kate a sleek sailing sloop with carvel-style smooth exterior. He may have basked in praise from his wife, but perhaps had private thoughts of an occasional poker game in Carcross with buddies from Conrad Mine and lakeside groups. The name they chose for their sailing craft was *Ben-My-Chree*, Manx-Gaelic language from the Isle of Man. As stated earlier, liberally translated into English, it becomes Girl of My Heart. The name had already graced the bows of more than one steamer serving Man.

In *Little Ben*, as Kate fondly dubbed her ship, the Partridges careened over Southern Lakes, where the stylish craft soon became well-known to miners, prospectors, fox farmers and settlers. Lake waters such as Bennett, Nares, Tagish and Mash washed the little sloop's keel. Winds from lofty ice fields filled their sails. They picnicked on beaches stepped by the rise and fall of lake waters, slipped silently into game-filled bays, pitching their tent in sheltered harbors, rising to up hook in scarlet dawns.

The Porter's log cabin at Ben-My-Chree. *Photo: Porter Collection.*

First glimpse of Ben-My-Chree at lakehead with glacier in the background. *Photo: Porter Collection.*

STR. WHITE HORSE IN FIVE FINGER RAPIDS

Steamer *Whitehorse* lining up Five Finger Rapids. Crew is shown winding in a greased cable by which the ship's winch hauled herself through rapids.

Photo: WH/YA.

Converted to oil and bearing a new Texas deck, *Tutshi* hauled crowds of well-heeled tourists. Here she shepherds *Duchess*, a small logging engine to serve a two-mile railway, Taku Town to Scotia Bay to Atlin.

Photo: ADC/YA.

Otto Hawker Partridge as a teenager about to leave the Isle of Man as a member of the Merchant Marines.   *Photo: Ron Tarbox.*

Cy Porter first saw Ben-My-Chree from the deck of the sternwheeler *Tutshi* in 1936 and later purchased in it 1971.

Photo: DD.

Pat and Cy Porter and Siamese Nui-Nui. For seventeen years the Porters strove to match Otto and Kate Partridge's open-door hospitality at Ben-My-Chree. How well they succeeded is reflected in the pages of their visitor books, now often browsed in their retirement home, Nanoose Bay, Vancouver Island, BC.

Photo: Porter Collection.

The seven who went North; left to right: author, Tsawwassen (dog), sons Kim and Russ, daughter Stephanie, Tok-tu-me (Siamese cat) and Pat.   *Photo: Porter Collection.*

Expanding traffic linked Carcross to Taku Town, a new Atlin Hotel and Ben-My-Chree.

Photo: ADC/YA.

Wooding up on the Stewart River. *Aksala* burned one cord an hour good steaming—more in swift water and lining.

Photo: DSC/YA.

Just prior to Closeleigh (Whitehorse) head of the hazardous Mile Canyon and the Whitehorse rapids, a landing formed the upper terminus of a wooden-rail tram. *Gleaner* and *Australian* dwarf little *Nora*. Photo: HC/YA.

Ho for the Klondike! By skiff, barge, canoe, even steam launch, they set sail on Lakes Bennett, Nares, Tagish, Marsh and LeBarge down Yukon River to Dawson.

Photo: YA.

71

Glacial silt slowly forms a sandy delta.   *Photo: Porter Collection.*

Swanson River winds ox-bow style from the glacier.

Kate Partridge's sloop *Ben-My-Chree*, built by her husband, marked the first use of the name beyond the Isle of Man. Kate sits astern and Otto coils a bow line as she lies stern-anchored off Engineer Mine.

Photo: ADC/YA.

The Partridge houseboat, built at Millhaven and moored at Ben-My-Chree. In 1912 she hosted a clutch of dignitaries, including (on the far left) William Brooks Close, the prime mover in a syndicate which built WP&YR railway. *Photo: ADC/YA.*

Shareholder Partridge managed the Bennett Lake and Klondike Navigation Co., constructing the "mosquito" fleet: *Ora, Nora* and *Flora*. A warehouse, office and living quarters adjoin Bennett's Dawson Hotel. *Photo: WH/YA.*

In May 1897, Otto Partridge climbed Chilcoot Pass to the tent city of Bennett. Klondikers waited by the frozen lake to launch jerry-built craft come spring breakup. *Photo: HC/YA.*

Top: Story-telling relics: an ore sack with Manx running legs logo, HBC butter box, lantern, enamel plate, cup and gum-boots with steel caulks. Atlin and Tagish Lake were believed to be part of Yukon prior to a boundary commission.

Above: Tipple cars, wheels and shafts still in grease-packed cases, are semiburied in spring-melt mud. *Photos: Porter Collection.*

Below: On the valley floor, overgrown by black alder, lie rolls of greased tramway cable.
Bottom: A clump of faintly smelling sulphur matches, a crumbling magazine, a shattered mauve-tinted whiskey shot glass, china chips and a tattered doily tell of life beyond the tree line. *Photos: Porter Collection.*

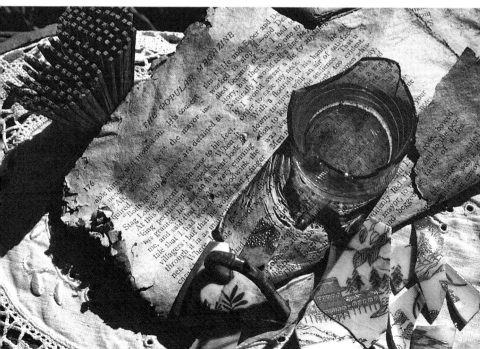

Lakeside friends in Ben-My-Chree garden. Back left to right: Swanson, Nellie Mearing (later Mrs. Bob Pelton), Otto, Mrs. Brook, Emily Dalton. Front left to right: Kate (with Jim Brook on lap), Miss Griswold, Miss Paula Gohacle.

Family winter travel, Squaw Point, Tagish Lake, enroute Carcross to Engineer Mine. Left to right: Walter Sotham, Mrs. Judy Brook, Baby Reg Brook, Jr. *Photos: ADC/YA.*

Awed by the contrast of culture and wilderness, world travelers never forgot Kate "Girl of My Heart" Partridge, her gentle charm, warm hospitality and little organ. *Photo: GMT.*

Almost level with a small valley across at Tusk's base. *Photo: Porter Collection.*

Clouds are mirrored in the lake far below.

Fall colors rim Tagish and a white skiff of snow cools the plateau.   *Photos: Porter Collection.*

Above: As *Tutshi* continued to haul hundred of visitors around the world, Otto and Kate's charm became famous.   *Photo: GMT.*
Right: Ludwig Swanson, whose name lives on in a Ben-My-Chree glacial river, late in life found a delightful young wife.   *Photo: AHSC/YA.*

Ben-My-Chree from the air in mid-October shows the delta outlined in frost. *Photo: Porter Collection.*

Looking down on the Ben-My-Chree homestead.

As years passed, Ben-My-Chree evolved with flowers, rockeries, greenhouses, a fountain and a wishing well.

Photo: WH/YA.

High in the mountains at Ben-My-Chree Mine, Otto Partridge holds his wife's horse; Emily Dalton leans on a walking stick and Stanley McLellan stands far left with his wife Annie.

Huge rhubarb, potatoes, carrots, cabbage and turnips grew swiftly in rich delta soil, aided by long hours of northern summer sunlight. Gardener Swanson is second from right.   *Photos: ADC/YA.*

By 1942 the Alcan Highway was well on the way. A pontoon bridge allowed traffic to move while a more permanent structure was built.

Photo: Pioneer Postcards, Kelowna, courtesy late Kay Johannes.

What a difference now! Driving through B.C. to Yukon in below zero degrees on clear pavement.

Photo: Porter Collection.

arly travel by road for e author and his mily was by Ford uck and camper. othing approached e economy, vision or daptability of this rig, though they saw any trailers, motor- omes and luxury odified buses. The can Highway in 1966 as not too bad. There as mud, dust and ad holes, but superb enery made up for ose little problems.
Photo: Porter Collection.

Stone Mountain Park sheep rambled across the famous military road and licked salt from our tires. *Photo: Porter Collection.*

The Porter barge at journey's end. Depending on weather and load, the journey from Tagish Post took a full day.

The swift way: a chartered Norseman loading at Tagish Post.

Photos: Porter Collection.

All supplies for building the Porter log cabin were barged 100 miles or more from Carcross, Ten-Mile Point, Tagish Post.

The beginning was rough-going, but a course or two brought smiles. *Photos: Porter Collection.*

Kim (hard hat) and the author—maybe as close to Heaven as he'll ever get.

After hauling and peeling, it was four feet to floor level, eight feet to eve and roll up to gable notch. *Photos: Porter Collection.*

Buttoned up so "grizzle bars" don't mirror other bears.

We thought a "gull-wing" would tiddly up
the roof. *Photos: Porter Collection.*

"Ah! She's in!" Fiberglass, massive, satisfying.

Roof on, hand-planed and facia trimmed. *Photos: Porter Collection.*

Marion Brook and son Jim view Ben-My-Chree's welcome sign following Kate and Otto's death. The words below: *Gratuities or compensation of any kind would be a desecration of the memory of the original owners. It is the wish of the Company that our visitors will enjoy the simple charm of this northern homestead as the personal gifts of Mr. and Mrs. Otto H. Partridge.* White Pass & Yukon Route. Photo: ADC/YA.

Creeasaurus, the last of its kind, guards the sandy delta at Ben-My-Chree. Photo: Porter Collection.

Yukon posseses a beauty which is unsurpassed. *Photo: Porter Collection.*

Chapter 5

Life on the Lakes

It now began to look as though Bennett City would revive and take its place as a solid community, perhaps in time rivaling Whitehorse, Dawson and Atlin. On July 6th, 1899, the railway reached town. Plans were in hand to construct twenty-seven miles through hard rock along the lakeside to Carcross, still persistently called Caribou Crossing by the railway, harking back to days when laying track across the White Pass was slow going. Despite freight delays entailing construction of a steel self-propelled barge to connect Bennett with Carcross, perilous blizzards and twenty-two-foot snow drifts blocking the rails, extension work continued. By July 29th, 1900, Carcross was reached. Preliminary work had been in process from Carcross to Whitehorse, but in the interim, steamers connected to Canyon City at the head of Miles Canyon, where now two tramways made yet another trans-shipment to Whitehorse for the final down-river passage to Dawson and beyond. Before long the railway would purchase the trams, eliminating that competition.

The mill at Millhaven continued to churn out ties for the railway by the bargeful. Kate Partridge entered into what might be described as her jam phase. She and Otto were out in the valleys and up adjoining hills and mountains, looking for wild berries. She gathered twenty-one pounds of red currants "opposite Lion Rocks." Next day this became red currant jelly, with an amusing little comment in her diary, "a leetle (sic) unripe."

August, 1902, saw her making seven pounds of blueberry jam, recording first raspberries, and collecting blueberries which became seven pounds of jam. She also writes, "have made altogether over sixty pounds of berberry and dried apple jam."

There seems to be no end to the enthusiastic energy of these two; the days saw them gathering a further seventeen pounds of blueberries, "also three ducks and five grouse." They were home at 8:00 P.M. and made thirty pounds of jam. Raspberries, blueberries piled up, with Otto whacking away up to his elbows in red and blue fruit. On Wednesday, July 27th, the two started early—got twenty-eight pounds and made all into jam before dark. One hundred and fifty pounds of raspberry jam contributed to a total of pails and kegs put away in the ice house. Total: 339 pounds.

They did not stop! When Otto was not jamming, he was dealing with an Indian who came in with six sheep. Cranberries became jelly presently; raspberries and blueberries seemed inexhaustible. Somehow Kate found time for fishing. In addition to numerous net and line hauls, one day she records, "caught 8 fine grayling—Swanson got 19." On October 11th, she writes, "For the past fortnight I have been smoking fish after salting from one to two days according to size. The *Alpha* (boat) men salt their fish in brine for 6 hours before drying outdoors. Flies do not spoil fish so treated."

Kate numbered amongst her friends a scattering of women whose husbands had elected to put gold-seeking behind them, turning their talents to raising grains, vegetables, even strawberries! She marveled at some bright souls who had taken advantage of a moment in fashion history when fox neck pieces were the rage. Today it is still possible to find remains of wire pens in little bays along Tagish shores.

When the two attended church, Kate often played the music. If organ or piano was unavailable, there was always the little Yamaha harmonium she had hired Indian packers to haul over the Chilkoot Pass, and now carried in *Little Ben*. The Partridges rightly came to regard these as glory days, loaded with excitement in, as Kipling put it, "filling the unforgiving minute with sixty seconds worth of distance run." Ahead lay the staking of more gold claims, creation of a working mine, financial disaster, even death, events which would shake their souls. Yet joy would be included in their destiny.

Back at Millhaven, the mill was enlarged and continued to produce. Cookhouse, storage and bunkhouse ashore in tents at the start, became wooden structures. Kate's diary reports Otto almost constantly on the move by steamer and railway, expanding his lumber business, managing revenue from *Nora*, *Ora* and *Flora*. There was tragedy in Kate's diary: "Poor Mr. Gray instantly killed in the mill at about 11:00 A.M. The saw caught a board and carried it back with terrific force against him."

The year 1900 at Millhaven was comparatively steady, Kate writing of what she considered as regular things: how Swanson fetched a twenty-five-pound box of candles from a cache at the head of the arm. They were almost out of light. It was January 3rd, and presumably kerosene had run out, supplies being difficult to obtain. Likely White Pass trains had become snow-bound, a common occurrence on the railway prior to introduction of rotary snow blowers. Each day provided a certain amount of excitement. Toward the end of January the diary reports, "Horse sick 2 days. Shot today." On May 1st: "Last night I saw the most magnificent aurora I ever expect to see—all over the sky and of every hue and color." She is referring to the brilliant Northern Lights.

The year 1901 did not start out as a good one. On February 7th, Kate's diary tells of a catastrophe which struck the tiny settlement:

> The mill was seen to be on fire at 10:15 last night. Swanson, Guthrie and Jamieson were in with us playing cards. The latter had spoken to the night watchman in the mill about three quarters of an hour previously. The fire was at work inside and nothing could be done except to save the lumber.

New machinery was immediately ordered, arriving by railway at Watson, across the lake. By September 9th, the mill was up and running, catching up on tie and beam orders. Kate tells how she and Otto were often out, once gathering seventeen quarts of wild cranberries. Christmas dinner that year rivaled any available Outside: grouse, potatoes, stuffing, asparagus, plum pudding, mince and apple pie.

From time to time, Partridge had staked several gold claims in Atlin and along Tagish shores by Bighorn Creek, above the gold camps of Hale and Kirtland in the lower Fantail River and Lake area, below White Moose Mountain. Not surprisingly, he continued to be attracted by the siren call of Ho for the Klondike! Feeling the blood tingle of adventure in a search for riches like crowds of other wild-eyed humans he had come to know amidst various businesses and along the trail. Common sense and a natural talent for commerce had shifted his mind in the direction of ship building and lumbering; but his heart still yearned for a chance to see for himself, to possess personally that magic known as gold.

Amongst the claims he examined with Stanley McLellan was one at the end of West Taku Arm, on Tagish Lake. Here the waters ended in a broad sand delta created by a surging river which bore turquoise-silted water, meltings from a glacier some twelve miles up valley to the west. He decided the claim had excellent prospects of a working mine. After all, Engineer Mine, only a few miles away, had produced considerable quantities and was still operating. When Otto told those at Millhaven about the gold, his companion Ludwig Swanson, wife Kate and her companion Emily Dalton were caught up in the excitement. The group wrote to Lord Edgerton, suggesting formation of a small syndicate to develop the claim. Now they needed to dispose of the mill, tow the houseboat to a slough site below the claim and use it as a base for operations.

What would they call the claim? Surroundings were beautiful: a sparkling sand delta, game in the valley, river and glacier presiding over a lush wilderness rimmed by snow-capped mountains. Otto Partridge felt the tug of earlier days on the Isle of Man. He suggested the same name as Kate's sloop: Ben-My-Chree, Girl of My Heart. His companions quickly agreed; the move was on.

Otto, Kate Partridge and Swanson initially lived at Ben-My-Chree in the same houseboat which had formed their home with Miss Dalton at Millhaven. Within a few weeks Swanson had refurbished an old log cabin ashore. This enabled the others to have a little more privacy and afforded him an opportunity to explore the valley and surrounding country. He assumed the role of wild meat provider, setting a trap line up valley and building another cabin toward the glacier, just beyond the first lake. A series of beaver sloughs provided summer access; in winter his dogs pulled a sleigh up the frozen river.

In time the river seemed to welcome him. It bears his name today. As a person, Swanson bobs up and down in Kate's diary, generally referred to as "the gardener," but he was more than that. He had been a simple laborer in the Bennett shipyard managed by Otto. A dependable worker, able and strong, he had accompanied the Partridges when they moved to Millhaven. He had become a personal friend and in time a partner in the Ben-My-Chree Mine. In middle age he discovered, wooed and married a younger, attractive woman, sometimes taking her on his trapline. Their up-valley cabin shows a woman's touch with shelves and washstand graced by patterned oilcloth, frilly curtains, a washtub and clothesline outside, and carefully kept grocery bills from Watson's General Store, Carcross.

As the claim became a mine, all was rush and bustle at the lakehead. *Gleaner* hove in view once a month, bearing mail, food, tools and machinery. It was an exciting time. Lord Edgerton came out from England, caught gold fever and rushed back to raise further funds, leaving a sizable sum behind as an initial share. Miners were hired, equipment ordered, including an aerial gravity tramline. Unloading pieces of the tramway (acquired from Conrad Mine on Windy Arm) and hauling the heavy cable reels, boxed axles, tipplecarts and other machinery across soggy marsh to a concrete engine base near the outbuildings taxed the camp's four-horse teams to their limit.

Stanley McLellan, who had shown Otto the claim, now left Engineer with his wife Anne, and assumed the position of foreman. He built a wooden, stone-ended building up in the mountains close by the mine, where the pair took up residence. Their home also became a dining room for shifts of the more than fifty miners who gradually swelled the ranks at Ben-My-Chree Mine. McLellan had become a full-blown partner in the Partridge-Edgerton-Swanson-Dalton Syndicate.

The settlement at Ben-My came to consider Atlin as their principal supply and social center, rather than the former Carcross. Kate encouraged Otto to sail their little sloop on regular trips to church and musical extravaganzas in the growing town. Otto, Ludwig and the miners kept an eye on Engineer Mine just down the lake, where regular sessions of poker stirred the blood and sometimes tempers. The shores of Tagish Lake in those days contained a substantial number of settlers, including a few women, who lent their talents and personalities to the nearest center of civilization, taking with them a variety of home-grown vegetables, small fruits, furs and sometimes surprisingly professional taxidermy.

In the years between the gold rush and World War I, particularly during summer months, life on the lake was anything but uneventful. Compared with Outside, many felt they lived by far the fuller life.

Chapter 6

Atlin and Ben-My-Chree

During days at Bennett City, Millhaven and Carcross, Otto had developed a healthy social and business liaison with the management of White Pass & Yukon Route, proprietors of the amazing railway which had confounded naysayers by breaching the White Pass and on to Whitehorse. The company had acquired and built a substantial paddlewheel fleet, at the same time buying out competitors who had driven fares down to the level of disaster. In the process of selling lumber to the railway Otto had come to be regarded as a man of vision—energetic and forceful.

At Golden Gate where Graham Arm stretched eastward to a tiny community known as Taku town, there was a tiny railway connecting with Atlin Lake, where another steamer linked to a town of the same name, and beyond to the area's gold creeks.

White Pass & Yukon Route had built a sizable hotel in Atlin, anticipating a flow of businessmen and visitors who now felt brave enough to see for themselves where gold was actually found. Those early tourists could now travel up the Pacific West coast from San Francisco to Vancouver in comparative comfort, and so to Skagway where a railway with astonishing scenery awaited. They could actually see from the train the famous Chilkoot Trail, where Klondike masses had struggled as part of the great gold adventure, enduring the harshest of physical and mental anguish.

On reaching Carcross, visitors could take a paddlewheel steamer side trip down Tagish Lake to Atlin. The return trip took them back to Carcross where a variety of Yukon and Alaska jaunts by railway and steamer awaited.

Atlin was an interesting community, created first by gold, and along the way adopting the title Little Switzerland because of its beautiful lake, mountain and glacial scenery. First gold was apparently known before the main gold-rush took place. Prospectors reaching Atlin in 1898 are said to have found the remains of early amateur mining sites dating back some fifty years before. Some speculate that before the United States acquired Alaska from Russia in 1867, adventurers from that country may have engaged in brief attempts to prospect the area.

In a delightful little booklet, *Atlin, 1898-1910: The Story of a Gold Boom*, there appears a summation of the breed known as prospector. This grand adventurer is described as the knight errant of a century that knew no romance. The prospector headed alone for an unknown destination. He was driven by an insatiable desire to see what lay over the next hill, across a nearby creek, or around an approaching bend; he pushed on, always seeking, seldom finding. If he was lucky enough to discover a rich deposit or creek he rarely remained for long at the scene of his find to develop the claim. All too often he died a lonely death on the trail. Only on strong arms, broad back and nimble wits could he rely. Little accidents on the trail assumed major proportions when he found himself far from doctor or friend. A wrong turn, a misstep, a sudden snow-storm or a rock-slide could bring serious hardship, injury or even death. He was frequently lost for weeks at a time. His precious supplies were often inadequate. He was exposed to all the dangers of forest fires, wild animals and the tricks of nature. Still he traveled on. If he succeeded for a short time he basked in the admiration of the mining world. Then, his brief moment of glory ended, he returned to his wilderness home. If he faltered or failed in his quest, he could appeal to no one for sympathy. He belonged to no union. He could not strike. He got no special treatment from any benevolent group of lawmakers or from charitable organizations. In his old age he was usually penni-less, but unlike his contemporary city dwellers, spurned the quiet life of easy retirement, in a center of civilization. He went on to the end of his days, and frequently died alone. Only some wild canyon or deep forest knew the secret of his death.

Fritz Miller is generally considered to be the first to discover gold in Atlin's environs. Miller prospected parts of Alaska and Yukon Territory from 1879 to 1897, visiting Atlin in 1898. Prior to that George F. Miller, a brother to Fritz, explored Pine Creek, finding traces of gold along that waterway east of the town in 1896. George Miller teamed up with his brother and Kenneth McLaren. Fritz Miller and McLaren set out by dog team from Juneau in January, 1898. They followed the trail over White Pass, but changed course east over the ice via Tutshi Lake and River to Taku Arm on Tagish Lake, and so eventually reached Atlin Lake.

From this minor start, a trickle of men to Atlin began; soon, as word of gold finds spread, the trickle became a stream, and the rush was on. In the summer of 1898, word reached employees working on the White Pass & Yukon Route. Groups of men soon formed, carrying with them picks and shovels belonging to the railway. Soon hundreds fled, heading for Log Cabin, a station on the new railway, and thence across country toward Atlin. Some 800 men stopped to collect wages, but many hundreds more charged into the wilderness on their way to what they believed was discovery of gold far in excess of monies due them for past labors.

Thus the men already working Atlin's creeks were soon overwhelmed by hundreds, then thousands of Argonauts, prospecting, staking claims and working day and night to extract the precious metal.

In town frantic building was taking place. Straggling tents soon gave way to office buildings, hotels, stores and residences. Several sawmills sprang up to meet a demand for lumber, their prosperity closely linked to ebb and flood of mining activity along the creeks.

But like many a northern community, Atlin was plagued by a series of fires. As stated in the Atlin Centennial Committee's publication *Atlin, 1989-1910*:

> On a windy Sunday afternoon late in August, 1900, Atlin had her first fire, the lessons of which she never forgot. A fire began in the warehouse of the British American Corporation and, aided by some kegs of blasting powder, which exploded, and a fierce wind, soon spread to the adjoining buildings.

The people of Atlin immediately began rebuilding, and also planned how to combat any such disasters in the future.

By June 1901, the townspeople had acquired a fire-engine, and established a fire brigade. Five years later the organization was severely challenged. On May 29, the town again suffered a disastrous blaze. Northern Power and Lumber's saw and planing mill, a quantity of timber, the town's electric light plant, steam laundry, blacksmith shop, office and quarters were destroyed, for a total of $40,000. The fire occurred on a Monday afternoon, washday, and the people of Atlin lost all their washing for a week.

Resiliency ruled. Rebuilding proceeded apace. Before long the hectic days of a brief summer season when the people were usually too busy taking advantage of every daylight hour to spend much time seeking recreation gave way to long, dark winter when citizens of the town pursued what fun was to be had. Societies and clubs blossomed. A branch of the famous Arctic Brotherhood was established. The group had been born on a Skagway-bound steamer in February, 1899, as a purely fraternal and benevolent organization, with its motto "Fidelity and Friendship," a watchword of "Mushon," and a miniature prospector's pan filled with tiny gold nuggets, as an insignia. The only bar to membership was that a member must have lived north of 54°. Even this rule was occasionally waived, as it was in August of 1909, when Lord Grey, Governor-General of Canada, his aide Viscount Lascelles, and Archdeacon H.A. Cody were initiated into Camp Dawson No. 5.

By the winter of 1902–1903 an operatic society came into being and after, expanded its scope to include a literary and scientific branch, purchased a piano, stage properties, and lighting facilities, and engaged the office and dining room of the Grand Hotel for its performances.

It was only a beginning. By October, 1903, the full-fledged and high-falutin' Arctic Club was formed by officials of the British American Dredging Company, who, it was reported, succeeded in causing associates in Philadelphia, New York, and Boston to subscribe $100 each to the organization. A 50 by 100-foot log building took shape:

Similar to the best club-houses of the Adirondacks in the State of New York...filled with books, pictures, banners, mineral displays, and photos donated by prominent business firms of Vancouver, Seattle and Atlin. The building contained a library of 100 books, and current magazines and newspapers, writing rooms, dining salon, a buffet, a ladies' parlor, baths, a piano, dancing facilities, a bar, and rooms for billiards and cards. A French chef had charge of the kitchen...the organization sponsored gun, hunting and fishing clubs.

Members included King Edward VII, Lord Roberts, Wilfred Laurier (Prime Minister of Canada) and Richard McBride (Premier of British Columbia).

An important link between Taku Town on Tagish Lake and Atlin Lake was a unique little railway. Prospectors initially slashed a trail bordering the treacherous and swift-running Atlin River. The trail expanded to something resembling a wagon road, later to become what was described as the world's shortest railway. In 1899, Captain John Irving and his Canadian Pacific Navigation Company hired some French Canadians to clear the route. Bob Pelton, onetime engineer of the line: "Where the hell he got them from God only knows! However, they soon got bitten by the gold-mining bug and quit their road-building job to swell the large number of amateur gold prospectors that had congregated in the Atlin District.

"Name of railroad, I believe is Atlin Southern, but local people always called it Taku Central. Length two miles and 1,000 feet: authority for this is V. I. Hahn, superintendent for White Pass, who surveyed the road when it came into possession of WP&YR in 1900. Mr. Hahn also told me the grade from Scotia Bay (Atlin Lake) to top of hill was steeper than anything on the White Pass line."

W. D. MacBride, a well-known Yukon historian contributed useful information on the railway, calling it the Shortest Railroad in the World. He provides a thumbnail sketch of Bob Pelton, recording how this adaptable pioneer graduated to roles of conductor on the (Taku) tram, purser of *Gleaner* and *Tutshi*, and eventually to agent at Atlin. He tells how the railway was purchased by the White Pass & Yukon Railway in 1900. A little logging engine built by Baldwin Locomotive Works in 1878 and used on Vancouver Island came to be known locally as the *Duchess*. She burned wood up to the fall of 1916, and was converted to oil in 1917.

The railroad consisted of a passenger car seating 48 persons and 6 flat cards of 10-ton capacity each. There were no turntables, so the return trip from Scotia Bay on Atlin Lake ran backwards to Taku Town on Tagish. At times the 7 percent grade required passengers to climb out of the car and push. Numerous amusing events occurred on the line. On one occasion a flat car jumped the track. Three husky prospectors, somewhat boozed up, crawled under the car and wriggled under an axle. By raising themselves on hands and knees, they managed to hoist their end of the car so that by working their own rear ends in unison, they eventually put the car back on track.

The first passenger car on this famous railroad was naturally air-conditioned with open sides. Swallows happily built their nests inside corners. When the car moved, the birds would fly alongside. The moment it stopped, they would enter and inspect their nests. A swallow sitting on her eggs would not move off at any time. Birds would catch flies during the trip, and fly to and fro with their beaks full of insects. Occasionally a fly or two, sometimes alive, would escape and drop down the necks of nervous ladies whose screams added to the already noisy uproar.

In the course of its adventuresome history the train was stopped by moose, bear and baby grouse sitting on the rails. Following robbery of a gold sluice-box in Atlin, all passengers and baggage were searched by the B.C. Police before they were allowed to board the steamer at Taku. Equipment broke down from time to time. *Duchess* was replaced by other engines. Finally, in 1937, the tram wound up pulled by a gas-driven truck, powered by a Ford V-8 engine and manned by a crew of three men.

Gold camps such as Atlin, Carcross, Bennett, Whitehorse and Dawson either faded or dramatically changed, inviting settlers, businessmen and tourists. WP&YR, enjoying a growing and profitable visitor trade, was able to fill their Atlin hotel where passengers happily bedded down on the shores of a beautiful lake surrounded by mountains rivaling anything they had seen in other parts of the world.

While traffic to Atlin continued, word-of-mouth news of a place called Ben-My-Chree drifted about in watering places frequented by the rich and famous. In fashionable resorts along France's Riviera, the Vale of Kashmir, on Caribbean Isles and by Lake Geneva's shores, those sipping delicate aperitif glasses were fascinated to learn of a mountain and lake gem where roaring falls, rivers and a glistening glacier made up a natural beauty seldom seen. It was said over two acres of immense flowers and vegetables were presided over by a cultured couple who opened their log home to all, and intelligently described their personal experiences with game, photography, almost self-sufficiency in the wilderness.

The tour to Ben-My-Chree commenced by boarding a narrow-gauge railway at Skagway, Alaska, riding over the famous White Pass, and in Carcross meeting a picturesque sternwheel steamer named *Tutshi*. Passengers were then transported up Tagish Lake to a beachhead, a view of a far-off glacier and close by a wild river with falls in the distance. Return fare including berth and meals was $15.

They would leave Carcross at noon, arriving by seven in the evening. After a guided tour of the property, which included a short walk to a three-tier falls, beavers and their dams in adjacent ponds, admiring the gardens, greenhouses and other log buildings, they would come under the spell of Otto and Kate Partridge and their generous hospitality. There would be organ music and singing, tales of the gold rush and hunting, steamer construction and exploration. Later that evening they would board the *Tutshi* again.

The trip often included a dance on the upper deck. Talented members of the crew included a pianist, guitar player and drums, often augmented by miner musicians from Engineer Mine, eighteen miles down Tagish Lake, if passengers included a goodly number of fair maidens.

The ship tied up from midnight to six next morning at the mouth of Tutshi River, where passengers went to sleep with murmurings of waters borne down from snow-capped peaks and pocket glaciers. They arrived in Carcross at nine next morning, returning to Skagway by train, or on to Whitehorse, Yukon, perhaps by steamer into mainland Alaska.

Thus a peculiar phenomenon came into being which in its way created an atmosphere almost as infectious as the rush for gold. It became the "in thing" to murmur a strange name: "Ben-My-Chree! Have you not seen it? Have you heard of a gold mine up there, and a tragedy too?"

In a short while the popularity of this oasis in the wilderness supplanted the alternate run to Atlin; WP&YR closed their hotel and devoted more advertising and energy to Ben-My-Chree. There had been times when the mine there was shipping ore, Otto and White Pass were at strong odds. Company freight rates were prohibitive. Instead of keeping their word to reduce those costs by ten percent, they raised them by that much. This put a severe cramp on anticipated profits, and Partridge complained bitterly. But after the mine faded, he met with field executives at Carcross and, on an experimental basis, persuaded them to open up a tourist route to Ben-My. He was a good promoter, an enthusiastic salesman, suggesting the company extend their popular route to Atlin to include their homestead. Already one or two passengers traveling the freight and mail run on *Gleaner* and *Ogilvie* had come ashore to be greeted by Kate, Miss Dalton and Otto.

Little did WP&YR's management imagine what a potent magnet Ben-My-Chree was to become. They were astounded how quickly traffic increased with each passing season. The legend of Ben-My-Chree became firmly established.

In exactly what year Partridge firmed up his initial arrangement with White Pass is not clear, but certainly the company assisted with financing and labor in many ways. As traffic blossomed, they sent in Japanese houseboys to help with Spring gardening. A team of wood-cutters arrived in the fall to take the sting out of winter wood-cutting and hauling.

The company expanded their assistance year to year as profits grew out of the operation. After the Partridges passed on in 1930, the company bought the acreage and buildings from the B.C. government, who had permitted the first founders to literally squat on their chosen place. Ludwig Swanson and his wife carried on the hospitable scenario of tours, music and the ever-present silver salver for visitors' cards, guest book and glass of home-made rhubarb wine. An electric light plant was installed. The whole place became a twinkling paradise as warm summer evenings drew a soft cloak about mountain peaks and up-valley by pond banks to the glacier. The long pier and steamer were illuminated by a chain of lights.

Chapter 7

Engineer Mine

Probably the main reason many prospectors prowled the shores of Tagish Lake, both before the discovery of gold at Atlin, on a lake of the same name, and in conjunction with the famous Klondike rush, was a group of hard-rock claims well toward the south end of Tagish, on what became known as West Taku Arm. The group was known as Engineer Mine.

Reginald Brook Sr., an engineer and geologist, managed this mine in its early days, and it is largely because of his well-written journal that we learn about this litigious operation. He describes the start of Engineer Mine with Charles A. Anderson rowing past large quartz veins running down into the lake. He stopped off to investigate, staking the Hope Claim and recording it in Atlin, on July 20, 1899.

Twelve claims in all were recorded that year, coming to be known as the Engineer Group. This name stuck through the years and was applied first by backers of Anderson, who returned with Henry C. Diers together with engineers who were putting through the White Pass & Yukon Railway. Some of the claims were staked in their names.

One of the outstanding personalities in the run of Engineer was Captain James Alexander, with whom Brook was closely associated from 1885 (when he was five years old) to his death in 1918, a casualty of the sinking Sophia off Canada's Pacific Northwest coast. Brook went to Engineer with Alexander in 1912, the two having had a thirty-two-foot launch built in Steveston, B.C., to cruise the B.C. coast. From time to time considerable ore was taken out, a two-stamp mill having been erected in 1910. Some rich ore was taken from the Double Decker vein, the first few hour's run reported to produce twenty-four one-pound plus eight ounces of gold.

Brook records some remarkable events, some amusing, others tragic, occurring during his tenure at Engineer. He tells, as an example, of an elderly miner, one Jimmie Stewart, who had been on a prolonged toot and was taking sulfonyl tablets to steady his nerves. They seemed to make him worse, so Captain Alexander took the medicine away from him and gave him five grains in the morning and at night, with enough drinks to taper him off. About the third day after arriving at the mine, Stewart took a walk along the lake shore beach to the mouth and did not turn up for supper. At around ten o'clock that night they went down the lake about two miles and found him pointing into the water. He said that some Frenchmen had attacked him but he had squared it all by giving his watch and chain to the women and children. There being no women and children within thirty-five miles, they knew by this he was well off his base, so after that Cap had Jimmie O'Neil watch him. Cap thought that if Stewart was employed doing something, he would be better off than moping round being sorry for himself, so he told him to set up the new assay balances. Jimmie O'Neil, who was roofing the bunkhouse nearby, shouted, and all ran over as Stewart fell to the ground. All they had to do was to get a whiff of his breath to know that he had taken cyanide of potassium. They gave him some mustard and water to try to make him vomit, but it was all over in a very short while. He did not live ten minutes. He had mixed a beaker of half and half cyanide of potassium and nitric acid, his last cocktail.

On the amusing side, Brook's journal relates how Cap Alexander and he took a fairly rich batch of gold down to Seattle, staying in the Frye Hotel. In order to draw the least attention to their treasure, the two decided to put it in a gunny sack, which was handed to the night clerk, with the request that he put it in the safe:

'What is it?' asked the clerk. 'Oh, a new kind of fertilizer,' I replied, seeking to divert any idea of value from it. I saw him put the sack into the safe and next morning Cap and I went to get it out. At the same time, Alexander suggested the clerk stash a bottle of rather good whiskey in the same safe. While the two were waiting for an assayer, they hid the gold-bearing sack under their bed, and went to breakfast. After making a deal with the assayer, Cap suggested they have a shot of whiskey. The assayer was astonished when the whiskey was found secure in the hotel safe. He had seen the gold brought out from beneath the bed, and told a friend that Yukoners were quite strange. Said he: 'Why they hide gold under the bed, but obviously consider good whiskey of greater value, for they keep it in the safe.'

Yet another entry in the Brook journal casually tells of a letter Cap Alexander received while out in Vancouver. The letter was from a Ben Nicoll, about a big man named Sam, who had gone out to O'Donnell River and was found dead on the trail. His dogs had sat over him for two months, but finally got a little hungry and ate up his insides and an arm. He was reported to be in terrible shape when they brought him in. Alexander remarked he had thought of having this chap cook for him the coming year, but guessed he would be cooking somewhere else now.

Engineer, being somewhat isolated, provided entertainment and sociability for the mine's employees and management. Otto Partridge from Ben-My-Chree, visited regularly, delighting in a poker game with Cap Alexander, Reg. Brook and Colonel Conrad of Big Thing Mine, Windy Arm. The Colonel liked to get Alexander into a good poker game. Cap was the only man around with any quantity of ready money, and they would play high stakes of $50 ante and the same to draw cards. If Conrad lost, he would give his check, which was sometimes good. If Partridge lost, his check was often not so good, and it was amusing to see those two swapping checks around, each trying to palm off one of their checks for one of Caps. The smaller tin-horn gamblers were sore because they were not able to get hold of any of Cap's money, being unable to enter the game owing to the high stakes.

Some years ago when first Marion Brook honored me by permitting a read of her grandfather's journal, I had a hard time crediting the following, which is undoubtedly the most remarkable true incident to occur at Engineer, and for that matter, at any mine! (Unpublished journal, Reginald Brook Sr., courtesy Marion and Jim Brook).

About the same time (September, 1918) our cook took a sudden notion that he wanted to travel as cooks so often do. This put us on the spot with a crew of men to feed. Cap asked me to go to Carcross and get another cook regardless of race, creed or color. It is about a 70 mile trip to Carcross, but I was back next day with the best I could get in the way of cooks, one Togo Fukuichi Hayashitani, Togo for short, who had promised me faithfully that he would work till the mine closed down at the end of October. Everything seemed to be going well till Togo complained to Cap that the steam engineer, Conrad Wawrecka, a former partner in the Northern Partnership, would keep worrying him in the early morning around 6:30 before the men came to breakfast, as Wawrecka had to get steam up by eight o-clock. Wawrecka, the Japanese told Cap, had told him that he would not be able to get along with Cap and stay till the last boat, because Wawrecka himself had not been able to get along with Cap at all. Cap told the Jap not to worry because as long as he did the cooking to satisfy the men, he would not come in contact with him.

Almost a week later, Wawrecka came to my cabin about 5:30 A.M. and excitedly told me that he couldn't get any answer from the Japanese in his cabin, and he had not got the cookhouse fire alight. I got up and went into his cabin and saw him lying in bed with his throat cut. I asked him what had happened and he could not reply but motioned that he wanted to write. I got him a pencil and writing pad expecting him to either explain what had happened and why, or to write his last will and testament, but he simply wrote 'Give me pistol.' I couldn't very well do this and told him he had already done enough mischief. I reported to Cap that Togo had tried to commit suicide by cutting his throat, but that he was not dead yet, so Mrs. Alexander, who was a qualified nurse, injected some Adrenaline to stop the bleeding.

Wawrecka passed Cap's cabin and said 'Too bad Togo had to go and commit suicide,' and Cap said 'You didn't help matters at all.' Then Wawrecka went semi-crazy, he jumped up and down and ended up by saying 'I'll fix you' and went off at a trot to his cabin. Cap said to me 'Go down and see what he is going to do and tell him to pack for Atlin.' I went down to his cabin and as I entered heard Studd say 'What are you going to do with the .22?' Wawrecka muttered something I did not hear and Studd said 'Don't be crazy, put that gun back,' which Wawrecka did. I told him to get ready to go to Atlin with me when I took the Japanese in. When I got back to Cap's cabin, Cap was standing in the doorway with his 20 Ross cocked and ready for action, and when one realized how he could shoot, Wawrecka would not have had much show to fix Cap if he had appeared with his .22 rifle.

We lifted the spring mattress that was on the bedstead and put it directly on the launch to take the Japanese to Atlin without disturbing him, then put it on a handcar over the Taku railway and across Atlin Lake in a boat we kept there for crossing when the White Pass & Yukon Route boat was not running, and got the Japanese to the Atlin hospital.

Dr. Hogan looked the man over and saw there was no chance to save his life, but said that while he still lived he had to do what he possibly could. As there was no anesthetist there he asked me to take on the job, and believe me the amount of chloroform I had to put on the mask was tremendous, possibly because the Japanese had a poor pick-up owing to the gash in his windpipe, and he seemed never to go under thoroughly. After the doctor had sewn up the jugular etc. around his throat, he proceeded to get him ready for bed and then he found that he had also cut right across his stomach, making a complete hara-kiri job of it. He lived till next day, but as we were in a hurry to get back across the lake that night, I made out my deposition regarding the decreased before he was dead to Mr. J. A. Fraser the Gold Commissioner who also acted as Coroner, etc., in Atlin.

When Stanley McLellan approached Otto Partridge at Millhaven and sought a grubstake (supplies furnished to a prospector on promise of a share in his discoveries) to further explore his gold claim in the mountains at the head of Tagish Lake, the principals at the mill examined the proposition with considerable interest. They had previously registered a number of claims in Atlin and along Tagish by White Moose Mountain near Kirtland and Hale, and still had high hopes of developing a mine.

Engineer is still going, albeit spasmodically. From time to time groups come and go, working for a time, then quietly drifting away, only to be replaced by another bunch. Once five women formed a little syndicate and whacked away in various tunnels, drifts and prospected high on the hillsides. Hope springs ever in the optimistic breast. When we visited, sometimes with friends, it was always interesting. Once we found a hippie abode along the shore. It was built of plastic, obviously abandoned. Inside was a fairly decent sleeping bag, soaked through, a rod and reel, a few bags of basic food such as beans, rice, oatmeal. Someone had been fleeing civilization. Who knows what fate had dealt him, or was it a her?

Chapter 8

Ben-My-Chree Mine

After examining McLellan's ore samples, the group felt the claim might prove minable. After all, Engineer Mine, only a few miles away, was producing gold. Partridge not only agreed to grubstake McLellan, but towed his canoe and supplies down to lakehead. Swanson accompanied the pair. After an examination of the claim, Partridge and McLellan struck a partnership. It was agreed McLellan, who held a foreman's job at Engineer, would build a large cabin at the mine and take up residence with his wife Annie, who would become camp-cook for miners when they were hired.

Back in Millhaven, it was decided to turn the lumber business over to the mill manager and arrange to have the houseboat towed to lakehead. They moored in a slough there, soon welcoming from England a hunting companion, Lord Maurice Edgerton. A former visitor to Millhaven, he was familiar with Tagish shores and mountains, having recorded gold claims in the course of hunting. On viewing the Partridge-McLellan claim, he became enthused and joined the group, leaving a financial contribution, and returning to England to raise more.

Despite the excitement of a possible gold mine, Otto and Kate Partridge left many fond memories of their sojourn at Millhaven. They recalled many expeditions into surrounding hills, up many rivers, exploring little known lakes. Two of these bear the Partridge name. At the head of West Arm the Partridge River runs in; further upstream is a lake bearing the same name.

Ben-My-Chree mine was not visible from the delta, but its general location could be placed beyond a mountain gully. A blazed trail led some 6,000 feet to the mine site. As work proceeded, the trail was improved to packhorse standard, down which ore in small burlap sacks was transported. Log stables were built below and horses brought in. When a few tons of ore were stacked at lakeside, the sacks were loaded on sternwheelers. *Gleaner* and *Ogilvie* hauled in freight, provisions, men and machinery, returning to Carcross with decks three deep in sacks. The cargo was transferred to rail and so to Skagway, with one more trans-shipment and an ocean journey to Tacoma where the ore was smelted.

Machinery for an aerial gravity tramway was purchased. Shipped to Ben-My-Chree, the heavy reels of cable, tipple cars and other components were laboriously hauled by four-horse teams across the delta to cliff base. Here a concrete foundation was poured to anchor the tramway. While this work was going on, one of the crew discovered an Indian petroglyph painted on nearby rock. It pictured canoes with sails, and indications of possible traffic by foot across the glaciers and snow fields visible at valley head, part of the Florence Range. More likely any travel into the area originated by way of Atlin Lake, Nelson and Edgar Lakes and the Wann River. This is one of the adventure routes some folks take today in the winter to reach Ben-My-Chree on skis.

An arrangement to assay ore samples was set up in a two-story log building below, where records and valuation of each shipment were kept. One of the interesting aspects of the original claim, similar to many in Atlin, was that this part of the country was first thought to be located in Yukon, and thus registered under the Territory's mining act. After finalization by an international boundary commission, these areas were placed, along with Engineer Mine and Atlin, in the Province of British Columbia. Size of the claims in B.C. proved to be considerably smaller, particularly the placers, with consequent dismay amongst miners and other owners. Organized protest, even riots arose in Atlin, were only settled by appointing an agent and making the fairest adjustments possible.

The original mine claim, and others traversing various sectors of mountains near Ben-My-Chree, are still carried on British Columbia mining records. Once during our ownership, we arrived to find posts and surveyor's streamers of scarlet tape marking claims across part of our land along the mountainside inside our eastern boundary. Unless dropped onto slopes by helicopter, the prospecting company would have boated into Ben-My-Chree's wharf, trespassed across part of the property, and so conducted their field work.

Today a healthy climber can trace an intermittent trail between screes and across gullies to the mine location. During our years we made welcome a group of young students from the geological faculty of Oshkosh University, Wisconsin, who regularly visited the mine as part of their curriculum. They camped near us on the delta and never failed to climb to the mine.

Once when we were cleaning out some older buildings, we came upon a three-legged figure carefully cut out of kerosene tin—the center of a stencil. The legs ran one way in a circular route. Later, when dismantling the crumbling Swanson cabin in preparation for construction of our new log home, we uncovered wet and mildewed ore sacks stacked two feet deep, used as ceiling insulation. Each sack bore the stenciled imprint of those same Isle of Man crest legs. We never found the actual stencil. The coat of arms had been adapted by Partridge who was, at least in his own mind, a loyal Manxman by education, if not by birth. His life of adventure, adaptability and courage undoubtedly was spurred on by the Manx motto "*Quocunque Jeveris Stabit*" meaning whichever way you throw me, I stand, a symbol of independence.

Gordon N. Kniveton, author of *The Manx Experience* has much to say about the running legs. He tells of research into the crest, a most ancient symbol. The oldest representation, he says, can be seen in the British Museum on a green vase dating back to the sixth century B.C. Similar to the better-known swastika, it is derived from a design showing the spokes of a wheel which represent the rays of the sun, the seat of Power and Light used in pagan worship.

Kniveton goes on to report that the three-legged design was taken to Sicily where it was adopted because of the island's triangular shape. Here the Vikings, during their excursions and settlements in the Mediterranean, came into contact with the symbol. Historians believe Alexander III of Scotland, whose son-in-law Edmund was King of Sicily at the time, adopted it when gaining control of the Isle of Man at the end of the Norse period of Manx rule in 1266. These are but a few of the variety of historical opinions existing. A personal note was provided to the author by Charlie and Muriel Tomlinson, Sicamous, B.C. who visited Ben-My-Chree. They subsequently wrote:

The most reliable version is that a Royal Princess from Wales met and married one of the first Manx Viking Kings, taking with her the Sicilian emblem which the Manx King and Nation adopted. It is said that at one time the people there claimed of the Three Legs: one knee knelt to England while the other two kicked Scotland and Ireland away.

Our expedition to the mine included my daughter Kerrie Des-Rosiers, her husband Denny, and myself. We made it up and down in one day. It was hard-going since part of the trail was obliterated. Our legs were close to rubber by the time they trod the delta again. We discovered short sections of the old pack trail crossing great boulder-strewn masses of loose rock, which moved ominously as we scrambled across. Eventually we stood where mine buildings once sheltered and fed the McLellans and a crew. After some eighty years of ice, snow, blizzards, freezing and thawing, avalanches and land slides, little is left of the mine workings. Some shredded planks, rusting tin cans, forlorn heaps of blacksmith nails and other debris lie spotted about. Just beyond is less than half a stone wall, all that remains of the humble abode where McLellan and his wife made their home. We poked about behind the wall and found several small chips of hand-painted china, all that is left of Anne McLellan's principal treasure. I put one chip on the wall and took a picture. We turned down the mountain, carrying with us a sadness which will always linger where once was human hope.

The Minister of Mines, Province of B.C., provides a record about the mine beginnings. It told how ten to nineteen men were employed in 1912 building roads and trails, buildings, preparing the ground and gathering timber for pylons on which an aerial tramway would be built. The minister felt from ore samples, there was every possibility of a mine. Claims on White Moose Mountain also looked promising. He deplored high freight rates by WP&YR.

The report made clear that all was in readiness for a vigorous mining operation when an avalanche and slide put paid to all hopes. The late Reginald Brook Sr. provides a short, and I believe factual report of the snow slide and tremendous rock avalanche in the spring of 1912. He begins by recording how just after a round of shots had been fired in the mine tunnel, a snow slide started and caught one miner, Vic Carlson, rolling him about roughly. He managed to keep on top of the slide, which swept through and over the cookhouse, killing Stanley McLellan and his wife. The balance of the crew escaped, as they were back at the tunnel mouth.

Walter Sweet and J. M. Ruffner, who had gone up to Ben-My-Chree in the steamer *Ogilvie*, told how the slide came down a depression where the cookhouse was built, and went right through, leaving both stone ends intact. McLellan and his wife were peeling potatoes at the time and were found, one with a potato and the other a paring knife in their hands.

One of the mysteries surrounding these events is the absence of reference in a daily dairy kept by Kate Partridge. She recorded much detail in their daily lives, including names of hens, number of daily eggs, kinds and weight of fish, size and weight of potatoes, temperatures, etc., but chose to say little about the mine disaster. It is possible she was so shocked, personally and financially, that she chose to keep to herself the pain and sorrow of this tragedy. She does record recovery of the McLellan bodies and their shipment Outside on the sternwheeler *Gleaner*, but nothing more, except for an exchange of letters with the deceased man's sister about disposition of a dog which survived.

Some years later a visiting journalist, Frederick Niven, having interviewed Otto Partridge, wrote a romantic article for the *Canadian Home Journal*. Niven states a snowslide began on the mountain and started a rock slide. Timbers of towers supporting the tramway were swept away and mine workings buried under tons of scree.

The journalist endeavors to describe such a rock slide. He says it was no little run of scree for a short distance. The rocks, like huge houses, were undermined by melting snows and the slide came down, bearing its weight against them. The result was cataclysm, havoc. There was a roar similar to tipping of a thousand trucks of steel rails. Boulders bound down, tracking a ragged course, wild, jagged and erratic, leaping sideways, cannoning into other rocks which were in turn activated. The slide carried all before it down Ben-My-Chree's mountainside, but fortunately exhausted itself just behind buildings below on the delta.

It is possible to imagine what it must have been like in the days immediately following the mine disaster. The bodies of the two McLellans were shipped out. Most miners were laid off. A few horses were retained, the majority sold. Two or three laborers remained behind to gather up tools and drill bits at the mine.

The area up there must have been muddy scree, shattered rock; immense areas of gravel and earth had been graded out in gullies and outcroppings, leaving a barren and silent expanse, no voices, no sounds of drilling, no smoke from a cheerful cookhouse chimney. The mine's main portal was nearly obscured, a scattered mass of tunnel props close by. Sadly the men must have slowly climbed down for the last time.

Some confusion exists as to the exact date when the mine was destroyed. The B.C. Minister of Mines lists the accident as October 5th, but this differs from the Brooks' journal, which is likely more accurate.

It seems the minister sought to put an optimistic face upon the future of this mine by stating that assay values obtained from samples of the ore were high, and that a sizable quantity had been sent to a smelter. Indications were that active development would be undertaken again as soon as the McLellan estate had been adjusted.

It was not to be so. There had been warnings about erection of the tramway a few months before. While some sixty-one miners were employed at the height of activities, the majority engaged in preparing to erect the aerial tramway supervised by J. H. McLean, a tramway engineer, some unforeseen difficulties arose, requiring guidance of a general mining engineer. That gentleman, after examining the site, pointed out problems might well be experienced because of heavy snow slides. He recommended the tramway be transferred to more promising claims on White Moose Mountain. This opinion gave the partners much concern; they decided to abandon construction and engage some twelve to twenty men under W.

H. Ireland to perform experimental work on White Moose claims. While these matters were in hand, the fatal slide occurred at Ben-My-Chree.

Down on the delta today, almost entirely overgrown by black alder, reels of two-inch greased tramway cable lie alongside cases of axles, wheels and tipple carts, all half buried in silt from years when the nearby stream overflowed its banks in spring thaws. No bolts exist in the concrete base to anchor heavy hoisting machinery. Perhaps the intent was to drill and sink methods of attachment later. An implement shed just beyond contains one complete tipple-cart, steel bearings and shafts greased and wrapped in burlap, still in an original packing case.

Not far up the mountainside it is possible to find crumbling pieces of wooden tramway pylons, rock platforms, occasional rusty bolts. Round about stand circles of hand-chopped pine stumps. How many pylons were completed we do not know. It appears construction of the tramway was well underway when Partridge's expert mining engineer recommended a change of venue.

Kate Partridge's diary records possible sale of the tramway machinery after the slide. Negotiations with Keno Hill Mine fell through. The equipment was left lie, until black alder and buckbrush mercifully blocked out the waste.

After the mine tragedy hard decisions had to be made. The miners had gone. Edgerton returned to England to lick his financial wounds. What should the little band do now?

They could return to civilization, leave the mountains, rivers and everlasting glacier brooding over a wilderness which seemed unlikely to change. But they all sensed a priceless peace. They had lost a goodly sum in the mine, but still had useful funds, enough to live reasonably here where there was little need for frills. The hills were alive with wild goat; up valley were moose, bear, the occasional caribou; sloughs and lake shore echoed whistling wings, the sounds of hundred upon hundred migrating geese, wild swans, quantities of ducks. Grayling made silent circles behind beaver dams. Gentle breezes wafted out onto level grassy land above sandy beaches where an almost level delta lay fertile, ready to welcome grains, natural hay and pasture.

They spent many hours that late summer sitting out on the barge deck, lifting eyes to the peaks which surrounded them. It all began to fit together: a background of fall colors, nature sounds, beauty, peace the possibility of almost self-sufficiency. A decision was made to stay put, as Kate's diary records, to abandon the tyranny of gold, to replace frustrations and noise of civilization with what they felt was an oasis of peace in the wilderness. Little did they realize where that decision, that dream, would lead.

Their friends and neighbors at Engineer, Atlin, Carcross and along the lakeshore would have been swift to understand, had they elected to go. They were familiar with the capriciousness of mining, excitement of strikes, despair when a promising gold vein dwindled and vanished. They knew of accidents and sickness, the end of a grubstake in what was often referred to as a hard land.

But Otto Partridge was not one to quit easily. He and Kate had fallen under the spell of Ben-My-Chree. So had they all. The four decided to stay, to move ashore, build a homestead and plant flowers and vegetables. They began to shape a wider dream than the original, to think on a world scale where wars raged; to share with others a form of gentle hospitality which over the years would embrace many, the humble, rich and exceptional of many nationalities.

They had experienced what the British poet Rudyard Kipling had penned:

Go softly by the riverside, or, when
You would depart
You'll find its every winding tied and
Knotted round your heart.

Chapter 9

A Different Kind of Gold

By the mid-thirties, steamer traffic to Ben-My-Chree created a waiting list of those anxious to book on the WP&YR steamer *Gleaner* from Carcross. The company, sensing a good thing, produced brochures picturing portions of Tagish Lake, West Taku Arm, the log buildings, gardens and a bright beach away in the wilderness. Plans were laid for building a new, larger paddlewheeler to be named *Tutshi*.

Otto and Kate Partridge, with Emily Dalton and Ludwig Swanson continued to be astounded as visitors trooped off increasingly frequent steamers. Shortly after demise of the mine, Otto had overseen finishing the log homes and outbuildings ashore. Now he sought to furnish and make more comfortable the two-story homestead. In time a billiard room would be added, lined with clear v-joint fir. This brightly windowed addition became the family's living room for all but the colder months. Soon a greenhouse adjoined a southern wall. A large pantry was added, plus a screened cooler outside, just beyond a corner window at the foot of stairs leading up to the bedrooms. A two-story assay office, some twenty feet toward the lake became storage for feed, a workshop and general supply space on the ground floor. Stairs led up to two bedrooms, which in time became quarters for houseboys.

Otto had ordered and planted potatoes. Carrot, beet, cabbage and other household vegetable seeds were on hand. Kate and Emily Dalton were busy choosing flower seeds and shrubs. The lean-to greenhouse outside their homestead dining-room housed raised wooden beds lined with galvanized tin, a water bib conveniently at hand. Earth was hauled in as was manure from the horse stables. In order to propagate seeds into plants, a small potting shed was built. Spring found the trio and Swanson planting seeds in their greenhouse. By the time seedlings were being transplanted into garden beds, Otto had complied with a request by the ladies and constructed a little screened gazebo above the original log cabin—now dubbed "Swanson's." Having watered the gardens, the group gathered up there as summer came on, to talk over the day's happenings, look out over the valley toward their glacier, or down lake over the delta. It was pleasantly cool after a hot day. The screens protected them from June's mosquitos and they often read and chatted through long summer evenings.

Swanson suggested a few hooks be installed in this elevated enclosure, so that game might be hung, protected from the flies. It was a good idea.

Miss Dalton, who held a special position in the household, occupied a private bedroom just down the hall from the Partridges' upstairs in the homestead. In early morning, she could look out her window and see Holyhead, a peninsula some five miles down lake. The point, which marked the beginning of Taku Arm proper, was named for a famous headland in England. Interestingly enough, the Ben-My-Chreeites always considered *up* the lake meant south from Whitehorse and Tagish Post. *Down* was north. Visitors considered the procedure strangely reversed from normal custom. But then they discovered that northerners, particularly Yukoners, were a peculiar breed. To live in this wild land they had to be.

Otto installed an ingenious water system fed through pipes from a tributary of the triple falls about 500 yards behind Swanson's cabin. A fountain soon sprang up amidst rock gardens, delightfully laid out with stone steps and walkways. Because daylight in summer extended well beyond eighteen hours, and the soil contained sifted volcanic dust to which was added a liberal dressing of horse and chicken manure, Kate's diary was soon recording swiftly growing vegetables of exquisite flavor, ten-foot delphiniums, pansies more than five inches in diameter. Visitors were hardly able to believe their eyes when they beheld a color-saturated profusion of blooms combined with grassy paths through vegetables twice the size found Outside.

Kate and Miss Dalton not only cooked daily, but bottled furiously, brewed jam from both domestic and wild fruits, and strove to deal with an abundance of wild game and fish brought in by the men. More shelves had to be built in the large pantry, and down below the homestead floor, a cellar ensured winter supplies would be protected from freeze-up.

All this time the volume of visitors steadily increased. The new sternwheeler *Tutshi* steamed down from Carcross three times weekly, bearing crowds of passengers. They poured ashore, first onto a walkway along the cliff base which led to gardens and buildings. Later, when danger of boulders bounding down screes above threatened ship and passengers, White Pass & Yukon Route built a long pier out across the sand to deeper waters.

Passengers had embarked on *Tutshi* from the Skagway train in Carcross and steamed 150 miles down Tagish Lake, arriving at Ben-My-Chree in the early evening. Two hours later, after having absorbed the unique beauties of this remarkable place, they returned aboard for the trip back, arriving in Carcross at 9:00 in the morning, after a dance on deck the previous evening, and following a twilight sleep and breakfast.

Their sojourn at Ben-My-Chree had first almost mesmerized all by an immensity of natural grandeur: towering snow-capped peaks, a rushing river, 4,000 feet of sparkling sand, backdropped by an awe-inspiring glacier. Having wound their way through a lush green arbor, they were greeted at a garden gate by Otto Partridge or Emily Dalton and taken on a tour of the flower-bordered rockeries, beside neat rows of rich vegetables, up a wilderness trail to the falls. From this elevated site they caught a view out over beaver-laden sloughs, Swanson River, and far off beyond two little lakes, a glistening glacier.

Back at the homestead there was Kate Partridge, elegantly dressed in black velvet, lace at neck and wrists. A silver salver lay on a side-table. Guests were invited to leave their cards and sign the visitors book. Glasses of home-made rhubarb wine were dispensed together with angel food cake and cookies.

Otto, a gifted storyteller, bon vivant, raconteur, held the visitors spellbound with tales of prospecting, hunting, life in the wilderness. It was then Kate's turn. Seated at the console of her little Yamaha organ beneath the flags of Great Britain and the United States, she played popular songs, inviting all to join in. Presently, she played a familiar hymn. The soft evening breeze wafted *Tutshi*'s warning whistle. It was time to go.

Those well-to-do visitors who had seen it all, who had chattered idly as the ship bore them into what they felt was just another odd place, now slowly strolled back aboard. They stood above a thrashing paddlewheel, viewing the glory of a northern sunset, feeling a sense of wonder, a mystical aura which enveloped their souls. As *Tutshi* moved across still waters, first one and then another light ashore turned on behind hospitable windows. Some passengers spoke of plans to return.

Toward the end of their two-month summer, the Partridges tidied gardens, overhauled their horse-drawn sleigh used to bring winter wood down from up-valley, and ordered final supplies which would be delivered soon by the last steamer.

Early frosts brought the snow-line on nearby mountains lower. A fleeting autumn blaze of birch colors began with greens mellowing into gold, then scarlet. The rather weary inhabitants of Ben-My-Chree thankfully slowed the summer's hectic pace. Petals began to fall from immense scarlet poppies, exposing rich seed pods, which were carefully packaged for use the next spring. Across the way, in the workshop-storage building, many tins of kerosene were safely stowed.

The women inventoried preserves and began to plan winter stews and puddings. Rhubarb was gathered, some bottled, the remainder converted into wine which would mature in barrels below floor level. Presently, as the temperature dropped, Otto and Ludwig Swanson glassed adjacent mountains for goats, seeking only yearlings, prime for tender fall roasts. With freeze-up, sloughs became windows of early ice. It was time to hunt up-valley toward the glacier, where a moose could be bagged, dressed and quartered, transported by sled to a meat safe outside the buildings, where it quickly froze. These were days when the team was hitched to a cutter and driven to previously cut cords of wood to be stacked beside the homestead.

They drew chairs up to heaters, brought out magazines and newspapers, letters from grateful visitors, swiftly read earlier but needing answers now. From time to time, prosperous visitors had sent in gifts such as a DeForest Crosley Radio, wheat grinder, radio transmitter and aerial, books and quantities of seeds.

Once during the Porter years of 1971 and on, we hoisted up a homestead trap door and gingerly stepped down into the cellar below, brushing aside years of cobwebs. At the bottom was a space about ten by twelve feet, with shelves along the walls. Beyond was a shallow crawl space. Our flashlight picked up something white far off in the corner. One of our sons crawled closer, discovering a pile of weekly Saturday Evening Post magazines, circa 1902–20, "5 cents the copy." We still have an August 28, 1915 issue, including such advertising gems as:

> The pocket Premi C. Kodak Anastigmat Lens F 7.7, 3 1/4 x 4 1/4, $17.00.
>
> Dodge Brothers Roadster, a dashing design, seats unusually wide, deep, generous. Roadster or Touring Car complete $785 (Cdn. $1,100, plus freight).
>
> Eveready Flashlight, $1.20. ($1.35 in Canada).
>
> Why his mother buys him BLACK CAT reinforced Hosiery. For boys and girls. Black, lustrous and dressy: 25¢.
>
> Bell Special Suit or overcoat, made to order, $13.50, Bell Tailors, New York.

Fascinating as these flashbacks are, best of all are the penciled initials "O. H. P." (Otto Hawker Partridge) on the cover, indicating the master of Ben-My-Chree had thoroughly examined each page.

Among the magazines and newspapers were *The Queen*, *London Illustrated News*, *The Times*. Summer visitors who met the Partridges for the first time were surprised to find in this far off wilderness a cultured couple, well-read, impeccably mannered. They marveled at the degree of happiness so obviously present in the midst of daily adventures in a land where lives often hung by a hair.

During winter months, which extended from mid-October to early June, the inhabitants of Ben-My-Chree settled into a daily round of activity, including self-entertainment. Every day wood had to be chopped and carried to the homestead, assay office and workshop. By about three in the afternoon lamps were trimmed and lit. After supper they frequently enjoyed a few hands of cards, or during the earlier temperatures of winter, a game of billiards in the front room. That portion of the ground floor was closed off by a sliding door as real winter set in.

Following departure to England of Miss Emily Dalton, after the mine disaster, her place was taken by a Miss Olive Ridgeway. She and Ludwig Swanson became friends and after a while married. This filled the gap of an evening with a fourth for bridge.

A few times each winter mail was brought in, either by Reg. Brook Sr. from Engineer, or by Indians on their way to hunt. In clear weather, Swanson and Otto took turns traveling on the lake to Engineer Mine, or by way of Hale and the Fantail Trail to Log Cabin, a station on the railway out of Skagway. When the lake froze, boats were stowed and another method of travel adopted. Kate's diary one winter makes note of her husband sailing down to Engineer, which may have referred to Otto donning skis, strapping a sacking sail framed by willow branches to his back and boldly shaping course for the mine. Swanson made regular forays along his trap line, staying overnight for a couple of days in his cabin toward the glacier.

Another daily chore was feeding the three or more horses which were housed in stables. Their stalls and remnants of attic hay remain to this day. Otto also spent time operating his forge. Homestead tools were shaped or repaired, a supply of horseshoes prepared. At other times he busied himself in the assay building, applying tools and workbench to making furniture and odds and ends for the home.

Evenings were Kate's time to tally up egg totals in her diary, and work her way through the yearly visitors book, remembering her guests by comments penciled in the margins. "Fuzzy Bobs" identified one; "large, dark, emotional" was another. There is little to indicate the fate of her chickens during winters, but likely they were killed in the fall, some eaten, others frozen for use later. She records a sizable incubation of eggs for a new flock each spring.

There was plenty of time to answer current mail, catch up on newspapers and lately arrived magazines. Some days were spent hunting quite close to the homestead, for mountain goats frequently moved down the mountains onto beach and flats.

As the years passed into the twenties, the Partridges felt their age restricting some activities. Otto had for years suffered from arthritis and a heart condition. Now on excellent terms with the transportation company, he was able to arrange for help with wood cutting, gardening and serving summer visitors.

In 1977, while camped at Taku Town with Peter Palmer, one of my real estate salesmen who had just purchased a piece of the acreage there, a power boat from Atlin arrived. Aboard was Harvo Inouye and Mrs. Takuo Inouye, wife of Takuo, who we were delighted to meet. The husband had worked for Otto and Kate Partridge and for Ludwig and Olive Swanson during the years 1927 to 1944. The Swansons carried on at Ben-My-Chree after the Partridges died in 1930. We learned that Takuo was living at Salmon Arm, and Harvo, a retired businessman, made his home in Toronto, Ontario.

On 9 September 1929, Otto Partridge applied to purchase the acreage known as Ben-My-Chree, but there is no legal record of their being registered owners. Considering that both Otto and his wife passed on a short time later, it may be that the previous arrangement whereby, with government approval, they simply squatted on the land, carried over during settlement of their estate. The land likely remained static until the B.C. Land Registry shows purchase by the British Yukon Navigation Company Ltd., on 10 February 1936 for $785.

Otto Hawker Partridge became seriously ill early in June, 1930, and was transported to hospital in Whitehorse, where he died June 28. Since it was early in the summer season, Kate carried on greeting visitors and extending traditional hospitality to all. The transportation company sent in help for the gardens, while Swanson and his wife provided whatever other help was required. These were sorrowful days for Kate. She expressed at one point during that summer her dislike for airplanes. "Only this morning," she said, "while I was feeding a moose calf that had become lost, an airplane noisily passed overhead, disturbing us both."

Fannie Kate Partridge did not have long to wait to join her beloved Otto. She too fell ill during the oncoming winter, was taken to the Whitehorse General Hospital and booked into the exact room her husband had occupied. She passed away January 10, 1931. Both are buried in the Old City Cemetery (south), in Yukon Territory's capital, Whitehorse.

What had this remarkable couple accomplished during their years in the wilderness? The North comprises an immense expanse of Canada, with comparatively few people. One might conclude that a single homestead, accessible by no road, not even a trail, would be of little consequence.

Instead the Partridges and their Ben-My-Chree linger on in the minds of a few still alive who knew them or about them. A great many more have come to know through records of parents who visited this scenic treasure surrounded by mountains and rivers in a lonely land. They have learned about a kindly and generous charm dispensed freely to all who came. Many visitors wrote, telling how the trip affected them, expressing thanks as best they might.

Elbert Storer, Agency Manager, Bankers Life Company, Indianapolis, Indiana, included, as part of his letter, a poet's quote:

There is a destiny that makes us brothers,
None goes his way alone,
All that we send into the lives of others
Comes back into our own.

Major P. K. Hodgson, Government House, Ottawa, Ontario wrote on behalf of Their Excellencies the Governor-General and Lady Byng of Vimy:

I am desired by Their Excellencies...to ask you and Mrs. Partridge to accept the enclosed photographs of themselves with their best wishes as a small souvenir of a most delightful visit and a mark of their appreciation of all your kindness and hospitality.

Mr. Walker Parker did not wait to reach home in New Orleans, but wrote from Hotel Vancouver, B.C.:

I have found hospitality in many lands, but to be the guest of a charming a host as your own good self, and in as snug a home as you have at the end of the trail and under the shadow of snow capped Ben-My-Chree is an experience I shall always cherish.

I hope that some day I may have the privilege of entertaining you in my New Orleans home.

Among hundreds of visiting cards which survive, Mrs. Myrtle Mullineaux, "Licensed Real Estate Lady," penned on hers a note, "I can see God everywhere in your beautiful garden."

What did the Partridges leave behind? They had set out to search for gold in a harsh yet beautiful land. Robert Service, in his famous poem *The Law of the Yukon* speaks about such as Otto and Kate Partridge, Emily Dalton and the Swansons.

Dreaming alone of a people, dreaming alone of a day,
When men shall not rape my riches, and curse me and go away;
...Dreaming of men who will bless me, of women esteeming me good,
Of children born in my borders of radiant motherhood,
Of cities leaping to stature, of fame like a flag unfurled,
As I pour the tide of my riches in the eager lap of the world.
This is the Law of the Yukon, that only the Strong shall thrive;
That surely the weak shall perish, and only the Fit survive.
Dissolute, damned and despairful, crippled and palsied and slain,
This is the Will of the Yukon, —Lo, how she makes it plain.

These splendid humans searched for and found a different kind of gold—that of giving themselves to others, and therefore receiving great joy. The Yukon Territory surely smiled on such as these.

Chapter 10

New Hands

I will never forget *Tutshi* and how she carried me from Carcross
down Tagish Lake to a place called Ben-My-Chree. That strange and
somewhat romantic spot with its beautiful gardens, surrounding
mountains and glacier captured the heart of an eighteen-year-old lad.
1938 was one of the years Canadian called the dirty thirties, colored
by doubts and fears. Parents were often heard to say, "When will it
ever end?" or "How are we to make the mortgage this month?"
Unemployment and worry were present in all ages. Elders worried
about getting or holding a job, any job. The young cast about trying
to discover what to train for. What would happen if parents were no
longer able to maintain a home?

In the midst of my teens, lady luck shone a warm beam. Yukon
became a temporary home. When Ben-My-Chree hove in view
something magical happened. It was as though a golden thread
attached itself somewhere inside, began to vibrate and stretch off
into an as yet unknown future. Something lay out there ahead,
beckoning. Robert Service, bard of the Yukon, puts it so well:

> Let us probe the silent places, let us seek what luck betide us;
> Let us journey to a lonely land I know.
> There's a whisper on the night-wind, there's a star agleam to guide us,
> And the Wild is calling, calling....let us go.

Perhaps you will recognize that golden thread in these pages. It is with my family still, and is likely always so to be.

Not until 1971 did the boyish desire to acquire Ben-My-Chree become reality. In those days we were operating a public relations company in Vancouver. One of our assignments was to find a candidate who could fill the needs of White Pass & Yukon Route for a public relations officer. I did not know Roy Minter at the time, but learned of his qualifications for the job. He had served in Whitehorse, Yukon, in the Canadian Army. He had become smitten with the country and its people. His particular love was the narrow-gauge railway linked in Skagway, Alaska with Whitehorse. One day he would write a scholarly book about that astonishing engineering feat: *White Pass, Gateway to the Klondike*. We recommended Roy, became good friends. In 1971 he tipped me off that Ben-My-Chree, dormant since 1955, was for sale. At the time we did not have much money, but that golden thread was still vibrating, so down I went to the bank and managed to borrow $10,000 as a down-payment. Somehow, over the years, while raising four children and struggling with various little companies, we managed to make the payments.

In the midst of the public relations project, Seven North, for the Ford Motor Company, Vanguard Campers, Honda motorbikes, Standard Oil and others, we briefly touched base with Minter in Whitehorse, and met George and Bea McLeod, then living at Tagish. In 1972, we drove up the Alaska Highway, hired a twenty-foot Hudson's Bay freighter canoe, powered by a 20-h.p. Mercury outboard. The McLeods suggested we park our truck and camper at their riverfront home. Then they offered to accompany us on the initial run to Ben-My, "so you don't hit every rock in the lake!"

Led by George in his homebuilt yellow cabin cruiser, bow high out of the water because of a heavy Homelite outboard, we chugged south on the lake, carefully marking George's route on our maps. First stop was Squaw Point, a sheltered north-facing beach, and favorite camping spot. A roadhouse once stood back of the beach, but nothing remains today. Round the point and along a little, we crossed from Yukon into British Columbia. The boundary can be clearly seen on either side of the lake as a tidy swath cut through the pines, winding up and gradually disappearing over mountains.

Talaha Bay to the east, once known as Moose Arm, was next. From the head of Talaha a trail once led to Atlin Lake. When we think of the convenience and comfort of today's boat travel on Tagish, it is difficult to picture hard-slogging prospectors making use of this route to reach Atlin's gold creeks. A river named Tutshi soon appears to the west, leading to a deep lake, similarly named.

Our map showed us to be abeam of Peninsula Mountain. We caught a brief glimpse of Racine Falls, a snow-white splash in the midst of lake shore greenery, gone in a second. We put into Potter's Point just beyond for a hot drink and sandwiches. In the days before Ben-My-Chree was established by Otto and Kate Partridge, the couple had many times sailed the route we now followed, slipping quietly into sheltered bays like Port Royale, so named by Otto for a harbor known to him during Caribbean adventures. The small inlet, where we lay to for the night, became one of our favorite stops, although the entrance was not easy to spot, particularly on rainy or evening forays. It was narrow at the mouth, shallow, curving, until suddenly opening up, there was a delightful surprise. The calm treasure offered several beaches, one good camping spot.

Once, in later years, when our aluminum catamaran barge was loaded beyond the Plimsoll mark with log materials, we sought shelter in Royale. As we cautiously inched our way in, there on the shore was a cow moose and calf, munching away in the shallows. The paradisiacal scene remains one of those memories which continue to be savored. Next day the McLeods led the way through a number of small islands to what is known as Golden Gate. Actually, there are two parts, Outer and Inner Gate.

Just a little to the east of Inner Gate, on Graham Inlet, we first encountered Reginald Brook Jr., his wife Marion and Jim, their son. They were a trapping family. In later years Reg and Jim built several log cabins which they rent out, part of Brookland's Wilderness Camp as it is known today.

More than anyone who knew Ben-My-Chree, the Brook family contributed to our knowledge of Yukon and our wilderness experience. It is difficult to put into words what they mean to us. Reg was a fountain of information, a mite dour until one burrowed in behind a gruff exterior to where the real man lived. On looking back, we appreciate his charity in putting up with our inexperienced antics.

Today Jim Brook, who seems to have always loved flying, has established Osprey Air with two airplanes. Largely self-taught as commercial pilot and geologist, Jim knows the country inside out, and possesses wide skills and experience in mechanics and maintenance. I have flown with many pilots up and down the B.C. coast and in Yukon, but I always feel comfortable when Jim is wheeling and dipping one of his craft up the narrow valleys, across lake and river, over everlasting snow fields and glaciers.

As the years passed, we changed our base from Tagish to Atlin, leaving our barge and some equipment at Brooklands. Jim took care of things, keeping our 85-horse outboard in fine shape. In return, we were happy to let him use the barge to bring in seasonal supplies. It was an excellent arrangement.

A short distance south of Golden Gate and across West Taku Arm, is an old-time abandoned settlement once called Hale. In 1898 it was a tent camp on the Atlin gold rush trail. After struggling over Chilkoot Pass, gold seekers once made their way across country toward what became Log Cabin station on the White Pass Railway. Following a variety of creeks, they finally rode Tepee Creek to a way point of the same name at the head of Fantail Lake, and so to Tagish Lake. Fantail was originally known as Otter Lake. This was the famous Fantail Trail used by Otto Partridge who traveled from Ben-My-Chree by skis in winter on Tagish ice, and then overland to Log Cabin to deliver or pick up mail and supplies.

Another abandoned site, Kirtland, links with Hale by a short trail. Here long-time trapline owner and prospector Fred Lawson and his wife lived for many years. Together with the Partridges, Lord Edgerton and others, they registered claims along Bighorn Creek. Some of these claims still show on topographic maps today.

Easily visible from this portion of the main lake is a perpetually snow-capped peak, White Moose Mountain, so called because of a remarkable likeness to a moose head, eyes, nose, face outlined in snow. It is a splendid signpost to all who traverse Tagish. Gold-silver claims on White Moose were also worked from a tiny settlement called Tatten Landing. Tatten has disappeared from current maps and thus becomes one of many names to fade into obscurity.

We stopped briefly at Engineer Mine where a few buildings remain, some in use by current operators. A building, complete with sign reading Butcher Shop is used as a cookhouse and tool shed. It was rafted from the abandoned townsite of Conrad on Windy Arm. Other original structures have been cannibalized; their interiors of clear fir V-joint have found their way to various cabins elsewhere, some far afield. The sizable stamp mill, originally built on a steep slope to the lake shore, took advantage of gravity to move ore through a variety of crushing and sorting machines. Near the lower mine tunnel entrances, one building for years teetered perilously at the edge of a pile of tailings. At last, having entertained many lake and air travelers, it elected to give up, and slid gracefully down to the bosom of Tagish.

Just beyond Engineer was an abandoned settlement named Hope. Although swallowed up by buckrush and decay, the name still persists on Federal maps. It was a good name for claims thought to contain gold. Next door southward is Wann River, the upper reaches of which at one time held a powerhouse and dam, providing power for Engineer. A couple of small cabins remain at the river mouth, leased by an American dentist from Juneau. Fishing for grayling off Wann remains prime.

Across Tagish at this portion of the lake is a major peninsula. Old-timers called this point "Holyhead," perhaps an attempt to civilize the wilderness by borrowing from Wales the name of a famous headland. In this final section of West Taku Arm, snow-capped mountains rise higher, pocket glaciers hang in alpine indentations; ahead stretches a clear arm. Far off and in the sky one can see a gleaming blue and white glacier.

As we approached the lakehead, we could see a river mouth, stretching out through lake-width sand. There was an elderly pier, jutting out through the beach to a docking area in deep water. Flashes of sunlight pointed to buildings. Sternwheel steamers initially docked close under cliffs far over at the right hand beach end, with access to property and buildings over a partially floating walkway. From time to time boulders bounded down from on high, endangering the ships. During the forties a long pier was built by White Pass & Yukon Route. It was quite an undertaking. Piles were driven into the sand for stability against spring flash-flooding from

Swanson River. There came a time when Ben-My-Chree acquired an electric plant. The pier was able to be illuminated, become a magical necklace of sparkling and reflecting lights, linking beach to ships.

We had arrived at Ben-My-Chree!

On our first trip, with Bea and George McLeod, we did not reach the end of our journey quite as we would have wished. At Holyhead our canoe met fierce winds and rising waves. Freighter canoes do not have a bilge; there is no space for water to gather except an area where freight and human feet rest. At the bow no chine forces waves to shy off, so wind-borne icy water blows back into one's face, cold—oh so cold! Pat, Russell and I were occupants on this trip. As we slowly buffeted our way toward a channel on the right shore, it became obvious the last lap would be miserable. That freezing water had made its way off my face, down inside scarf and feather jacket. I began to feel muddle-headed, the beginnings of hypothermia. I shouted to Russell up at the bow, "We're going to make a run for it. Better buckle down. When we hit the shore, tear out and make a fire!"

Russ, who was a well-trained boy scout, understood perfectly, although he was just as cold as Pat and the skipper. I opened the Merc throttle, and we smashed through sizable waves, leaving McLeod's craft astern. Dimly I remembered steering close to the right hand bluffs. There on the sands, right in front of us was our welcoming party: a cow moose and calf. They gazed peacefully at us, the mother leading her little one slowly into neighboring brush.

When at last our bow hit the sand, Russ jumped out, ranging about like a hound-dog, in search of dry twigs. Pat helped me ashore. I was barely able to stand. Wet boots, jacket, shot of over-proof rum and all, somehow my two helpers got me into a sleeping bag close to the fire Russ had miraculously built. Half an hour later we were able to take stock of the dream from thirty-two years ago when I had last seen Girl of my Heart.

We walked up the old board path, now overgrown on the sides by black alder. Some of the planks were pretty shaky, but soon we came upon remnants of domestic flowers, blue delphiniums and bachelor buttons mingling with crimson fireweed. A faded sign, with the words "Welcome to Ben-My-Chree," with a set of moose antlers fronted the old gardens. The fence was mostly down, but still protected patches of huge domestic poppies and lupines.

There were the buildings, graying, with roofs tattered and torn, roofing askew. No maintenance had been done since 1956. In the homestead, two stories, we set up shop. There was an elderly barrel heater and a battered cook stove. Furnishings included a much-worn chesterfield, dining table and benches, pantry, chiffonnier, kitchen table and several built-in shelves. We made the best of this dusty domain, hauling groceries and other gear up from the canoe, helped by the McLeods who had by now arrived.

I remember walking upstairs in the homestead and finding a white, brass-trimmed double bed in a room where Otto and Kate Partridge slept. There was a wooden washstand with enamel basin and china water jug. I looked out through rusty window screens to the mountains. By opening the window and leaning out I could see a beaver dam, partly flooded meadows and glimpse a glacier.

This was a room of forgotten voices; soft conversation at day's end, man and wife chatting gently together about important happenings; perhaps the need for an even larger woodpile to fend off another winter; a planned meat hunt next day; the weather; the latest world news described in a lately arrived bundle of papers, including *The Illustrated London News*. These were well-read folk. Not for them an outcast life in this far-flung outpost of Empire. They might have left the man-made uproar outside, but not the culture of their upbringing, the desire to maintain a standard of life worthy of the beauty which now surrounded them.

In subsequent trips north we formed the habit of lying quietly in that historic bed. We sought to relive large lives under a roof which was now ours. Then the twilight deepened, a friendly and cool breeze wafted down the valley and made music through our window screen as it must have years before. Faint intermittent sounds of falling water were the last sounds. A magical morning awaited.

The first night was exciting. A colony of mice had taken possession of what was once a spotlessly clean home for Otto and Kate Partridge and Miss Emily Dalton. Barely had we lit candles than little scurryings began. With startling boldness, hordes of four-footed varmints scampered from dark corners, scooting over our feet, into food packages, up onto tables. How we wished we had brought one of our cats from home! Pat threw together a quick supper. Soon we were snug in our sleeping bags. I made the mistake of winning a toss for the chesterfield. Hardly had I closed weary eyes when through my hair, down across my ear and nose zipped a curious wee mousie, eager to size up this warm body who had invaded his home. Pat and Russ were also treated to strenuous mouse explorations. The McLeods bedded down on their cruiser where they slept the sound sleep of mariners. For us there was not much rest that night.

Next day we prowled about, examining the old Swanson cabin, an ancient structure with tiny lean-to at the rear. It was in almost total decay with roof sagging, pithy logs, barely habitable. An implement shed (sans roof), stables, blacksmith shed including anvil and blower, completed the structures. All buildings needed immediate reroofing if we were to halt decay caused by leakage of rain and snow melt.

During following days we explored boundaries of the property, working from an original survey. Otto Partridge had originally squatted on this land, ignoring a British Columbia Preemption Act of the day, seeking instead to establish residence, erect buildings and prove through the government agent in Atlin his right to a form of pioneer ownership. He, like many who adventured into this wilderness, viewed ownership of the land as a form of reward for having braved exploration and planted "the flag" as a beginning of civilization.

The agent and some influential friends in Victoria were sympathetic, and for a while it seemed likely the idea would materialize. But then, as now, those in government feared a precedent. Finally, Partridge arranged for Horace McNaughton Fraser, B.C. Land Surveyor, to examine the Ben-My-Chree land. He prepared a survey, using a scale of one inch to twenty chains, each chain comprising sixty links of a foot each. To begin, he had to establish a starting point astronomically, having no neighboring property on which to base his bearings.

Although later in life I was to enjoy partners who were surveyors in land development, I always admired their ability to plunge into a wilderness and bring about order where none had existed.

Fraser traversed along beach, across slough, river, mountainside and meadow, creating 156.85 acres which he caused to be registered as Lot 4684, Cassiar District, B.C. Thus Ben-My-Chree became unique as a legally surveyed and recorded lot on Tagish Lake. Since those days very few such surveys have occurred up there, and because of a long-shelved hydrographic plan which established a reserve on lake and river frontage throughout the watershed, it is likely to be one of the last. There may be demands beyond Canada for more water, more power, but as long as the bulk of Canada's populace clings to a narrow band of climatic comfort along her 49th parallel, Ben-My-Chree will continue to preserve her quiet beauty.

Although we had full field notes showing posts and traverses, we were unable to find many boundary posts. We were not surprised since over forty years had passed. Moose and other wild game had trampled posts. Many such markers had been set in flooded moose meadow, others on the Swanson River bank. The meadows had been flooded and reflooded thanks to the efforts of beavers, nature's finest engineers. Swanson River showed every evidence of shifting course as annual volume of water from glacial and snow melt exerted pressure against banks and timber, creating new gravel bars and sloughs. At the river mouth sand and silt had created an immense delta, in movement year by year.

Exploration was great fun. We climbed a short way up the north bluff. Here were remains of an old packhorse trail, leading to the Ben-My-Chree Mine which we had to leave for another year. During our initial possession tour we were content to gaze out over magnificent scenery, reminded of a quote from a 1920s White Pass & Yukon Route brochure which read in part: "Notice that the upper end of Tagish Lake is the true start of the Yukon River." We had read a variety of claims to this honor, but were quite prepared to accept the pioneer transportation company's assessment. It was exhilarating, after all those years, to find my family owners of this storied wilderness homestead at one of the very beginnings of waters on which I had earlier sailed in sternwheelers.

We managed to thrash our way through heavy brush and black alder along a steep mountainside to reach a cascade of three falls. Later we used a minor rivulet as drinking water. From half-way up the first falls, we looked out over miles of moose meadows, beaver dams and ponds toward the glacier. Two shallow lakes had been created by the Swanson River, which itself was now visible in a series of ben-bows.

Suddenly there was movement in the meadows. A cow moose, undoubtedly the lady who had greeted us earlier, stood quietly feeding. What breeze existed wafted from the moose to us, so she just kept on munching. Her calf was not in sight. We worked our way down, coming upon the remains of an old road shown on the survey plan as being used by the Partridges to haul in wood with the first snows. Presently we found signs of a domestic water system: an elderly metal cistern, three-inch galvanized piping running off in the general direction of homestead and gardens. Then we came out at the rear of Swanson's cabin. We were home.

In time we would dismantle that building, but now we rummaged about inside. A battered heater stood in one corner, table and chairs, but the real treasure was a well-preserved Captain's bed, taken from one of the steamers. For many a year the roof had leaked badly. We stood on a table and pried up a ceiling plank. Two feet of soggy ore sacks greeted us.

This was the oldest structure, occupied by Ludwig Swanson, great friend, partner and employee of the Partridges since their arrival in Yukon. Before that, Stanley McLellan, who prospected and jointly claimed what became Ben-My-Chree Mine, likely bedded down here. Beyond that we do not know. In the lean-to behind we found prospecting gear, a pick and two shovels, the blade of one worn almost in half from many an hour of shoveling hopeful gravel.

In the course of our ramblings amongst the buildings, we uncovered all manner of treasures: shafts and bearings wrapped in original grease and burlap; chimney pipes, wire on which were threaded various nuts, wooden boxes of bolts, shanks of rope, lengths of chain, all manner of pipe connections.

In subsequent trips members of our family hiked neighboring mountains, including The Tusk, a major mount across the lake. This area included several pocket glaciers, feeding streams which thundered down in the roar of falls. The sound lulled us to sleep pleasantly each night. Once my son-in-law Denny DesRosiers and Russell, packed an overnight kit and climbed to the base of The

Tusk. It was quite a struggle, working first through dense timber, crossing and recrossing the wild falls as they cascaded over bare rocks, at times falling hundreds of feet below. They made camp in an indentation at Tusk's foot. In the night, wind and snow attacked their tent. Although they had used rocks as tie-downs and packed the tent perimeter solidly, at times they feared a blowaway.

Russ was enamored at the time of a young lady named Laurie. In the morning he climbed to a bare plateau and labored to haul rocks from quite a distance. With these he spelled out the young lady's name. The romance did not last. I often wondered what helicopter crews thought as they flew overhead prospecting sites for gold and other minerals.

On our second visit to Ben-My we decided to travel from Tagish in two small canoes, using an outboard and towing the other canoe. Both canoes and a host of gear went up the highway by truck. The ever-helpful McLeods provided several ten-gallon cans for gas, space to park the truck and camper and their usual brand of hospitality. On looking back, some force for good was watching over us on that trip. By the time the canoes were loaded, with Pat, Denny and I in the lead craft, daughter Kerrie and son Kim in the tow, we were a mite overloaded. So long as Tagish remained reasonably calm, all would be well, but if it blew? We would have to see.

Just out of the river and barely into the main lake, we faced mounting waves and had to take to the beach. We pitched tents and hunkered down for a frustrating day. The wind increased, three-foot waves crashed on our beach. We despaired of making the first lap to Squaw Point. Eventually things calmed down a bit and we took another shot at it. All went reasonably well, our loads decreasing little by little as we cached full gas cans on islands and in bays, ready for the return trip. Kim and Kerrie were an easy tow, mainly because we used nylon rope which gave somewhat in rough spots. After a day, we made Brooklands and took a breather.

Morning came and we were off again. Once round the corner and out of Graham Inlet that wicked wind began to whistle down the lake. We felt it best to shape for the far shore, hoping to find a lee. The waves really set our teeth on edge. I strove to quarter each one, varying the throttle to ease blows to both canoes. Heavy spray, then real chunks of each wave began to come inboard. There was an old lard can for bailing, but when water in the canoe began to get ahead of my bailing, I knew we were in trouble. The water, as usual, was ice cold, and although every trick learned through years of boating on B.C.'s coast was used, those inland waters were a different breed. Waves were short, steep and breaking. We barely made the far shore with two inches of water in the lead canoe. The other canoe fared better, but Kim and Kerrie could not be faulted for questioning the skipper's wisdom. Who could blame them? We were all soaked to the skin. A quick fire and hot soup never tasted so good. We needed another form of transportation.

Every year down in Vancouver we never failed to enjoy the annual boat show, particularly since we were engaged in ocean-front development. Boating was an important part of our lives. As Pat and I strolled through the show, she happened to notice an aluminum catamaran houseboat, used mainly on lakes and reservoirs in B.C. and down in neighboring American states. "Why don't we adapt those pontoons and deck for use on Tagish?" she asked. That turned out to be, as we often laughingly reminded each other, "a rush of brains to the head!" We obtained details from a Winnipeg firm and ordered two twenty-four-foot pontoons with connecting brackets to attach decks. We bought marine plywood, gave the sheets three coats of marine enamel and prefabricated what came to be known as "The Porter Barge."

Pontoons and fastenings were shipped to Skagway, then by White Pass to Carcross, where George McLeod picked them up with his truck. On our next trip to Tagish, we assembled the craft which measured eight feet wide and twenty-four feet long. At the rear we assembled a 4 X 4 foot shelter, with Plexiglas windshield. Unkind spectators dubbed this our mobile outhouse, but it did the trick, leaving room to service and gas an 85-h.p. Mercury outboard.

Now it was easy to pick up a couple of forty-five-gallon gas drums in Whitehorse, roofing and other materials, load onto the barge by Tagish bridge and off up Tagish River to the lake. We found the craft able to handle most weather, although from time to time waves broke over a half-sheet of plywood placed at the bow to act as a spray guard.

Each year we made the trip, camper and sometimes trailer journey up to Prince George, west on Highway 16 to Kitwanga and up the Cassiar Highway to a junction with the Alaska Highway just beyond Watson Lake. The highway was still pioneerish in early trips, banked and winding. Once we came round a bend and there was a trailer split wide open, end to end, festooned with a wedding trousseau, bedding and other gear. A little way ahead, parked carefully as far off the gravel road as possible, was a mud-encrusted Cadillac. No one was around, but we surmised bride and groom were gathering their shattered nerves together in a near-by lodge.

Despite mud and dust, we enjoyed these trips which eventually wound up by way of Jake's Corners to Tagish. The lake trips were a dream. We created a canvas cover for the barge, disposing of the outhouse. We included windows all round the cover, screened against bugs when we moored in bays along the way. We were able, in good weather, to make Ben-My in a long day, taking advantage of twilight summer nights.

We tackled the roofs of buildings as an initial project. Sometimes it was necessary to replace planks where damage had been extensive. We used ninety-pound mineralized roofing and the task of measuring and packing the heavy rolls was a challenge.

One summer, when our whole extended family came up, we chartered a Beaver seaplane. After loading the usual mass of groceries, building materials, and a brand new wood stove for Pat, I asked our bush pilot how we were doing for weight. "When the pontoon rudders go under water, Cy," said he, "I begin to worry a bit. Last trip we piled her up a bit much. Had to throw out a pack or two, but we managed to get her off!" Sometimes it is best to let the experts handle finer details, and just shut up.

Another strenuous session saw us ship in so many rolls of that heavy roofing that, in the interests of time, we had to charter an extra Cessna 180 from Whitehorse. When she arrived, those rudders were certainly well down.

Pat was overjoyed with her new stove. We off-loaded it from the seaplane into a small aluminum boat, then up the slough and man-handled her into our homestead building. Later it would be transferred to a new log home.

These one- or two-month tours were possible because we had been fortunate in acquiring the services of a young lady whose name was Wendy Fuller. She had answered one of my employment ads for Pacific Shore Realty. She was only sixteen and courageously told me that in spite of this being her first job she felt capable of filling our need for a Girl Friday in the office. She turned out to be a quick learner, and with accountant Pat's help soon proved her worth. Within a few years we elected her a director of the company, and left her in charge of office and salesmen while we went North. Any fears I may have had at first soon melted away; with Wendy in charge, salesmen went their best lick and lawyers watched their step. When we returned sales were frequently higher than had we stayed at home!

When we elected to trek North in mid-June everything on the lake was fresh and green. At the mouth of streams snow was piled high. Fish were anxious to bite. Game was everywhere. Tiny islets held hundreds of nests, many filled with chicks. All who ventured close were dive-bombed by anxious bird parents. A large disadvantage on shore were clouds of mosquitos and little black flies. At Ben-My-Chree we were fortunate in having a flow of glacial cool air whistling over our buildings which discouraged the bugs. That same wind gathered momentum beyond the beach, building short sharp waves at Holyhead which discouraged visitors in canoes or kayaks. If we happened to be watching, we would see visitors brave the point, but often turn back. Those who did make it, we welcomed. Ben-My-Chree grew in our hearts in direct proportion to the joy we experienced in sharing this beautiful place with others. As a family we decided to maintain, as fully as possible, the hospitable spirit displayed by founders Otto and Kate Partridge. When in residence, we opened wide our doors, kept the kettle boiling and tried to keep a healthy jar of cookies and cake on hand. During the times when we were absent, winter or summer, doors were left closed but unlocked. Outside the homestead was this sign:

Use things as you need them;
Leave things as you found them.
Thank you, The Porters.

Inside we left plenty of kindling, paper, wood and matches in case someone got stuck at lakehead. On our shelves were basic foodstuffs, dehydrated soups, tea, salt, biscuits, cutlery, pots and pans. We quickly discovered visitors, whether from Yukon or Outside, were keenly interested in Ben-My's history. So, like Otto Partridge and his Kate, we tried to have early-day yarns ready to tell, a story or two from founding times.

One of the most popular groups to come our way journeyed the long distance from Oshkosh, Wisconsin. They were geological students from Oshkosh University, who, with their leaders Professor Tom Laudon and son, sought our permission to camp on Ben-My acreage. We were delighted to welcome both young men and women. Expert campers, they were polite and congenial, lapped up our stories and were eager to help in any way. They had made the long sojourn to examine Ben-My-Chree Mine, climb adjoining mounts and screes, where many geological formations lay ready to be explored. We liked to watch through hunting scopes their energetic climbs back and forth across canyons, streams and cliff sides. Well-known to the Brooks for many years, the students wrote field examinations at their home.

We maintained a visitors book in the Partridge homestead. Each year the pages filled with men and women from far off places, just as in the beginning. Some were returning after many years; for others it was a first trip. Although we could not meet all boats, we sometimes sensed one or two tiny specs down at Hollyhead. But most of the time a brisk wind blew across Ben-My from the glacier, keeping their sound away.

There were occasions when Pat and I found ourselves alone and enjoying every moment, although to see family and friends depart was always sad. One morning we launched the canoe on our slough, above the first beaver dam, and turned toward the glacier. We hauled over twelve dams, some better than ten feet high. Everywhere channels led off into alder and willow stands. Occasionally we saw eager little pioneers gnawing away at a tree or towing branches to their conical homes. We frequently heard the sharp crack of a tail on still waters signaling the animal's displeasure. Occasionally, when we let the canoe lie motionless, curiosity overcame fear and one or two beavers moved closer and closer until intent little faces peered up at us from only a few feet.

After a husky few hours of climbing and hauling over dams, we came to the first lake, paddled across and made fast. Our children had reported geese and a host of ducks on previous journeys. An overgrown trail led along the shore. Little piles of bear scat appeared. With some trepidation we pressed one. Nui-Nui, our Siamese cat, riding on my shoulder, fluffed up his tail and growled, aware of a whole host of new smells.

We crossed a vigorous stream and below, toward Swanson River, was an abandoned trapper's log cabin. We struggled down and discovered the creek had changed course, now flowing right under the cabin. Inside it was touch and go as we explored where a floor once existed. Everything was exactly as the owner had left it: a tiny cookstove, ax, cross-cut saw, pots and pans, some dry groceries on shelves. Carbon copy of a grocery order for oranges and potatoes lay on oilcloth by a washbasin. They had come from Watson's General Store, Carcross. On another shelf stood a tiny bottle of strychnine, a poisonous alkaloid once used in trapping, now outlawed. We climbed outside again, convinced by washtub, clotheslines (and shelf oilcloth) that the tin-roofed abode had known a woman's touch.

How had the cabin stove and other heavy gear found their way to this lonely spot? Had it been laboriously paddled up as we had come? More likely the owner had waited for freeze-up, loaded a sleigh and urged his dog-team up the frozen Swanson. Later we learned from the Brooks the cabin had been built by Ludwig Swanson who from time to time trapped up here, sometimes with his wife for company.

It was time to retrace our steps. As we neared our canoe, Nui-Nui set up quite a howling, obviously scenting something strong, perchance a bear. I scrambled over a beaver dam, untied our craft. Pat was right on my heels, now carrying the cat. To my shouts of "Hurry up" Pat replied, "Well, it's your bloomin' cat!"

Over the years various members of our family joined us. Some came up by truck and camper, others flew to Whitehorse and either air chartered directly, or met us at Tagish for a long lake trip. We never experienced an idle or dull moment. Dozens of projects presented themselves, such as trimming lower pine tree branches to expose Partridge rock gardens, pools and fountains, wishing well.

One year our long-time friends Grace and Phil Ballam of Victoria joined our caravan. It was a year when we drove to Atlin, then flew to Brooklands, boarded the barge for Ben-My-Chree. Phil had been a scout in the old St. Mary's Troop, Oak Bay. After a day or two orientation, we decided to brush out a former trail to the falls. All went well, even though hacking down thick willows and throwing them aside was not the easiest of tasks. By the time we viewed the falls in all their splendor and worked our way back to the cabin, we were certainly tired.

Phil declared he always left something behind on his treks, so that his appreciation could be marked. What did I need doing? I mentioned a door to the sail shed, and Phil was off and running. He announced need for a chisel. It was found we were chiselless. This caused quite a hullabaloo, for to an ancient plumber, not to have a chisel was absolutely inexcusable. He made do with a sharpened screwdriver and hung a craftily made door which swings noiselessly away up there where the wind blows cold. Because of all this commotion concerning a chisel, we dubbed Ballam "Lord Chis." To his chagrin the name stuck.

On another tour, we lowered the old flagpole, painted it a sparkling white and replaced rope and pulley. It was quite a puff and grunt to bring her upright again. Soon a new Canadian flag snapped at masthead. Thereafter when in residence we always hoisted the colors. Visitors of earlier days told us that to see a flag once more flying at Ben-My-Chree brought back happy memories of Partridge days.

It seems appropriate to wind up this chapter by poking a little fun at the Porters. One trip included Pat, Russell and myself. We air chartered, landing on a lake of high water which covered our sand delta. The pilot felt it wise to let us off at pier end. The pier itself was elderly and had many gaps as it crossed over flooded areas.

We unloaded extensive supplies and gear in the teeth of a strong cold wind, and bid the plane farewell. A long stretch of muddy water separated us from shore. Circumstances seemed to indicate a raft. We cannibalized pier planks, lashed them together and launched Russ at the end of all the rope available. Quite a distance from shore he ran out of tether. His next voyage included much electric wire also contributed by the pier. That was not enough either, so back we hauled the intrepid adventurer. By now dusk was coming on. We decided to bed down out there in the wind and cold. So, up with the tent, nail her down with considerable muttering and perishing fingers. The night was restless.

Up betimes. Just as we were about to launch expedition three, Pat happened to stand a two-by-four in the water. Yes Virginia, it was only twelve inches deep! Embarrassing? You betcha! We pulled on heavy socks and boots, loaded backpacks and made the first of many wet marches to shore.

The toes were wizened, but no quite so severely as our egos.

Chapter 11

Log Cabin

As the years passed, we managed somehow to pay the taxes on Ben-My-Chree. Payments had to be scrounged for White Pass & Yukon Route, from whom we were purchasing our northern dream. We seldom missed an annual pilgrimage, traveling in and out, up and down the Alaska Highway by truck and camper.

The parade of roofing rolls, tar and nails continued. One by one, each building received a snug cap, becoming more visible from the lake. Some were red, others green, depending on availability of supplies in Whitehorse. At times we neglected to record the roof color for a certain unfinished building, so that occasionally we wound up with a "Christmassy" two-tone job. We could not ignore these color wobbles, but secretly hoped visitors would not circumnavigate each building on initial exploration, and might so fail to notice our slip!

We continued to bed down in the old homestead building, but the girls, particularly Pat, began to be a little restless with what they felt were inadequate cooking and washing facilities. We bought a brand new cook stove in Whitehorse from Taylor and Drury, that much-favored pioneer supply store whose name brought back fond memories. I had met Bill Drury in company with Pierre Berton when we were about to begin the great Yukon adventure years ago. We stood together beneath a cedar tree arch in Vancouver's Stanley Park and had our picture taken. In later years, Charlie Taylor, who managed the Whitehorse store, made sure I had a warm feather parka, boots and gloves, and never failed to put on a friendly smile. Like Howie Firth, one-time Mayor of Whitehorse, and his wife, these were salt-of-the-earth Yukoners.

The stove was trucked out a few miles to Schwatka Lake, seaplane base for Whitehorse, and manhandled up into a seaplane. That was the easy part, although at the time we thought it quite a struggle. Then away we went up over Tagish to Ben-My-Chree. There the lake was low, sand stretching out over the delta. We had to off-load into a small aluminum boat, well off the shallows. The stove was heavy, expensive, and to us a precious treasure.

Have you ever lowered something like that out of a rocking airplane, inch by inch, knowing that one slip and not only would the prize be lost forever in icy waters, but carefully husbanded dollars shot? And who knows how many tasty, home-cooked meals lost?

At last we managed trans-shipment, paddled to the slough safely, hauled the beauty up onto a bank and with many a grunt and groan slowly wound our way up an overgrown pathway to the homestead. The women were overjoyed! Pat supervised installation and immediately prepared detailed instructions on care and cleaning of the stove's gleaming surface. Hand-printed on a piece of cardboard and hung close by, the rules were pointed out to all visitors. Woe betide anyone who failed to apply a paraffin coat after use.

Even after scrubbing floors, walls and ceilings of the old homestead, it was obvious the ladies would appreciate better quarters. Despite our best efforts plugging holes and setting traps, when we retired each night a whole tribe of little furry creatures scurried about the homestead. They came out as soon as it was dusk, boldly crossing our feet, up onto the table, across food shelves. When we tried to sleep, they ran over our heads, even down into sleeping bags.

Our Siamese cat, Tok-tu-me, went his best lick, filling his tummy, but had to acknowledge defeat after an hour or so. The numbers were just too much. He lay in midroom, growling in frustration, while meal after meal scurried past.

We spent some time prowling about the wonders of Ben-My, carefully examining each building and eventually decided to dismantle the oldest cabin. It had been built by unknown pioneers during prospecting days. Unrepaired many years, the roof leaked, log walls sagged and floors had rotted away. We held a family conference and decided to dismantle Swanson's cabin and built a new log home on the old site. It had by far the finest view of any building on the property, high, well-drained and commanding a magnificent overlook down the lake.

Pat rose to the occasion and came up with a simple but effective plan. We have always had a rule in the family: I pick the land and choose a site; she plans the building. She probably should have been an architect. All our homes have been designed by her, in whole or in part. Our best, designed by Walter Wiltshire, an architect from Edinburgh, Scotland, disciple of the famous American Frank Lloyd Wright, rested on ten acres of Gulf Island oceanfront. It was a beauty and Pat, as foreman of works, was right on the job, and deserved much credit for livability in the final result.

My contributions to the new structure were mainly logistic. A rough lumber and log mill was operating at Ten-Mile Ranch, not far from Carcross on Tagish. I wrote owner Dave Harder, enclosing Pat's plan and asked for something akin to a prefab procedure, logs to be of the sausage variety. That meant they were to be run through the mill in uniform eight-inch diameter, flat on two sides in our case, rounded on the remaining two. Floors would be two-by-ten-inch rough pine joists, roofs two-by-eight.

Partitions would be log, but of a smaller diameter. Others items from near and far included double-pane wood frame windows which we found presented not only considerable expense, but a challenge to transport.

Down in Vancouver, we had expanded our real estate activities to include a cedar home franchise, with three display cottages on acreage in Richmond. We had developed several commercial contracts and it was relatively simple to shop wholesale windows. By the time crating, taxes and freight were included, the final cost to Whitehorse was fierce. Then we faced transport down the lake. About that time, one of the family spotted what looked like a suitable set of windows in a Sears mail catalogue. They were made in Quebec, of pine, included screens. Best of all, the price was much less than our B.C. wholesale and, believe it or not, the whole could be f.o.b. Whitehorse, crating and freight included. On top of that there was no sales tax in Yukon! We were off and running. In due time the windows arrived in Whitehorse. When we pried open a crate to see what sort of produce we had, they turned out to be prime.

While all this was going on, I had ordered 100 pounds of twelve-inch galvanized spikes, which raised the eyebrows of a Whitehorse merchant! Other supplies included bales of fiberglass for log chinking, partitions, cement, roofing, rigid insulation, shiplap plywood. We lined up a large aluminum freight barge, rented in Whitehorse. Two Native friends agreed to search out and bring to lakeside three forty-foot log purlins. We would be responsible for towing them to Ben-My.

Down in Vancouver we assembled a power plant, tools and a host of odds-and-ends. Finally we headed up the Alcan with two daughters, two sons, two dogs, two puppies and one cat. Daughter Kerrie's dog Miche had presented her with two round balls of fluff-and-chew, so the entire menagerie had to be included.

We boys—son Kim, son-in-law Denny and I—rounded up gear in Whitehorse with our truck and arranged to have the barge trailered to Carcross. But not before Kim stepped into the mechanical breach and repaired an abused inboard-outboard engine which powered the barge. We had picked up the windows in town, and with gear and tools of all kinds, set out for Carcross and launched the barge for a trip to Ten Mile Point. Loading began there, but after the sweat of yarding logs abroad, there was no room for lumber. The roof and floor boards would have to travel later on our smaller barge. Materials supplied by Harder were good but his dock and foreshore left much to be desired. There are always a multitude of tasks to be done in the short spring-summer-fall season up North. Generally, only the most urgent receive attention. After running the ranch, mill, machinery and home, not much time remained at Ten Mile for docks.

We had to painfully hand-load each log, after wading out in the coldest of water. A brisk wind whipped up the lake into sizable waves. The job was far from pleasant. In the midst of this, there was a startling diversion.

The ranch dog, a large collie-type hound, stepped on a triple hook fishing lure which someone had left lying about. The lure was large, intended for good sized lake trout. When we finally cornered the howling beast, removing three hooks from a paw was quite a challenge. The dog, suffering intensely, turned savage. Only after we threw a wet potato sack over him and literally sat to hold him down, were we able to tackle those curved hooks. They had pierced the foot pad with two prongs. Cutting pliers failed to sever the hard metal, so we resorted to a hacksaw. Unfortunately we had no anesthetic. It took a long time. And the dog fought with all his strength. Eventually, covered with blood, earth and dog hair, we were able to pull the hook out backwards, and bind up the foot. The episode had been traumatic for all hands, but at least it warmed us up for another battle at log loading.

When we shoved off into the waves for Ben-My, barge pontoons were barely above water. We plowed up lake, motoring through the summer night and arrived safely. Later the girls and dogs arrived in our barge, loaded down with food, tools and other gear.

We had dismantled Swanson's old cabin the year before and now brushed out and leveled a somewhat larger space on the original site. Then came operation concrete. We carried sacks of cement about a quarter mile from lake shore. To find clean sand and gravel meant taking our barge across the Swanson River delta to the far shore where a stream tumbled out of the mountains. Here we shoveled and screened a mix into tubs on the barge. Back at the wharf, we hauled up to the site. We had brought up from outside a length of some 600 feet of black plastic pipe This we strung through the bush to a small waterfall where we built a dam. Soon running water was available to mix concrete for the foundation pads.

We were a bit shy on laying out experience, but had studied building manuals and listened to contractor friends. The task of batter boards, leveling up, squaring and form construction proceeded apace. Kim and his wife Cheryl had taken on the task of unloading and carrying logs, one by one, from the slough up to just below the site. The wood had been seasoning for three months and while somewhat lighter than when cut green, was still heavy. Some logs measured twenty feet.

The first course was square on all four sides, firmly bolted down to foundation pads. In succeeding courses, we drilled holes every four feet, each log hammered down with foot-long spikes. We agreed this was one building which was not about to go anywhere. It may even have passed through our minds that what we were about was the erection of a personal monument there in our wilderness.

Fiberglass insulation was cut into strips by the girls who then bostitched them to logs as we laid and spiked them. A gas-powered electric plant, powersaw and squares speeded up cut-off work and fitting logs to pre-planned window and door spaces.

Four of us, Pat and I, daughter Kerrie and Denny her husband, were the construction team. Kim and his wife Cheryl had to return to Vancouver, so Pat and I took them down the lake. We called in to Ten Mile Point on the way back and picked up an overload of two-by-ten floor joists. On the way, we had what we would always refer to as our personal bear adventure.

Prior to that trip we had worked twelve-hour days, only pausing twice for short meals. While Pat and I were away, the Kerrie-Denny team whacked away, finishing walls and starting in on gables. When we came back, they set out in the barge for Tutshi to fetch purlins. These were fir logs each about twenty inches at the butt, eight at the tip. They were recently felled, green and immensely heavy. Kerrie and her husband faced the formidable job of towing them about seventy miles on Tagish Lake. As my son-in-law put it, "Tagish decided to rattle our cage!" They fought their way through more than three-foot-high waves. Several times the tow rope broke. That meant rounding up the logs on a rough lake, retying, and on once more. At last they put into our friends the Brooks at Golden Gate, warmed up and borrowed a length of dog-team cord which stood up until Ben-My. By that time we were more than a little worried. When at last they arrived we plied the doughty travelers with many hugs and hot drinks.

Now the real fun began. We had raised walls and gables, but faced moving those heavy purlins from lake shore to cabin and then up onto the sloping gables. Den is a genius when it comes to practical problem-solving. Face him with an almost insurmountable task and he noses about after a solution like one of his dogs after birds.

This he did at Ben-My. Together we sniffed out mine wheels, sled parts, axles, pipes and miscellaneous mine fixings. Soon we had constructed what we affectionately named "Log Lover." It was an invention which would have brought joy to any lumberman's heart: two flat-tired pulley wheels on a short axle, the shafts from a horse-drawn sleigh, and a cradle crafted from rough pine planks. On this we were able to set the smaller end of each purlin, enabling navigation of curves in the bush trail to site.

But first we levered and jacked the heavy logs up out of the lake onto land, then higher up onto our walkway. George McLeod, our willing Tagish neighbor, had loaned us one of his special creations, a three-wheel tired cart onto which the heavy butt-end of each log was hoisted. Then it was brute strength with block-and-tackle away up the walkway. It took a day for each purlin to reach cabin site, another day for peeling bark, and yet one more day to hoist, inch by inch, each log eight feet up the outside wall, plus a sloping roof gable.

We cut notches halfway on each gable and at the ridge. When each log reached its allotted notch, and was pried slowly into place, there was a satisfying thunk. That brought a combined "Ahhh!" from all the troops.

It was a great adventure. By the time we were ready to lay, level and plane roof boards, we had become intimately familiar with the principles of lever, pulley and gravity. We had dredged up long-forgotten elementary physics and geometry and learned to use block-and-tackle almost to the point of professionalism. The women played a major and essential part. After each heave-ho on the tackle, they made ropes swiftly fast, securing the few inches gained. We would have been lost without those extra hands and smiling eyes.

One purlin, when hauled to the gables, proved to be about four inches further to cabin rear than desired. We pondered the problem of shifting that massive weight without lowering down a fearsome ramp, to say nothing of losing time and energy so painfully gained. Sometimes one has a little luck. I found an old rubber washing machine roller in the brush. We levered up the purlin end, ever so carefully slipped in the roller and pry-barred the log forward. It worked! We still have the roller.

While part of our team were fetching purlins, Pat and I built stone foundation pads for the floor, putting in two-by-ten pine joists. We used two-foot cut-offs as braces for a strong grid. Now there was a skiff of early September snow high on the mountains. It was time to leave. Hurriedly we fitted windows and door into trimmed openings and built detachable window covers from salvaged boards saved from the original cabin. We had been counseled human vandalism would not be a problem but grizzlies disliked their image in windows, frequently smashing, then entering unoccupied cabins.

Smack on the dot of forty days from a standing start, we stood back and admired the gullwing roof, smartly painted white windows set deeply into log walls, bright green mineral roof. Earlier in our marriage Pat had told me she would love one day to have a log cabin at the head of an inlet. It turned out to be a fresh water rather than salt, but now she was a happy woman.

We had a day available before making connections in Whitehorse. Our young people chose to present us with a surprise canoe tour of sloughs opening upvalley. They insisted on acting as hosts, doing all the paddling and hauling over beaver dams. The trip was not altogether new, but luxurious in that we enjoyed the fun of doing not much but relax and enjoy. Beavers came and went; ospreys screamed and dived overhead; ravens wheeled and swooped, greeting us with raucous indignation.

Eventually we reached the first lake and prowled along game trails amongst fall colors. As usual, the air was fresh and pure, a gentle breeze following the Swanson toward Tagish. On the way back all was still. Small beaver tributaries wound away to their conical houses. We reveled in the peace of mountains and pocket glaciers, and the generous spirits of our first-born daughter and her husband.

In 1977, Kim joined us to complete the floor. Over those heavy joists we set two inches of rigid insulation, with shiplap joints in two by four squares; then a heavy gauge vapor barrier of polyfilm extending up interior walls an inch or two. As a finish floor we used half-inch plywood, whose joints we carefully caulked. Two coats of white marine enamel topped it off. We installed smaller log partitions, created an entrance mud room, kitchen-living area, food storage space, bathroom and bedroom. We had rescued the precious captain's bunk taken from the original Swanson cabin, and now installed it with due ceremony.

We installed a hand-built double bed toward the front of our new home. Now we could lie and look out over stables, sand delta and away down to Sentinel Point with its tiny islands in West Taku Arm. An original Partridge wicker arm chair and two tables on casters from the homestead completed furnishings.

Carpentry that year was to have been accomplished with a portable power plant, but try as we would we were unable to get the brute fired up. Eventually Kim diagnosed the trouble. Our spare parts kit failed in the clinch. My son faithfully hand-sawed every matching piece of floor plywood. It was an arduous and painstaking task tackled with cheer.

Looking back, I realized our entire tribe had absorbed a family virtue sometimes laid down rather forcefully from the head of our dining-room table at home: "Stick to it, and press on!" The lesson stuck as a family motto.

The following year, son Russell and I installed an insulated metal chimney, moved mother's stove up from the homestead and put in a sink, drain and grocery cupboards. Pat was in her element. Everything was spick and span. Great bustlings began amidst flour, pans and the like. Presently there arose the entrancing aroma of home-made bread. There followed a roast of beef—rare, delicious. Wood stoves produce a flavor like no other in this old world. This was indeed the life.

At other times, in other years, we gathered wild raspberries. Within a few yards of the cabin we were able to fill a large bowl. After we had gorged ourselves on their tanginess, Pat turned more into jelly, raspberry vinegar and pies. The vinegar was one of her Scottish grandmother's recipes. When mixed with Ben-My-Chree pure water, this was a royal drink.

With completion of the new cabin, we found an additional incentive to visit our wilderness retreat. The structure was a great success, snug, bright and inviting. We had done it all ourselves and were justly proud. Our closest neighbor, Reg Brook, boated up with his wife Marion and son Jim one day, allowing as how our cabin was "pretty good," high praise indeed from such as he.

Reg and his family were fine friends with great stories to tell of a full life on the Southern Lakes. When Reg Jr. passed on rather suddenly, it brought home to us how swiftly Canadian history slips beyond our grasp. If we fail to set down what may at the time appear to be ordinary daily affairs, particularly in the Canadian North, surely we short-change our children, to whom early struggles are fascinating. To our grandchildren they are astonishing; to their children, almost fictional. Continuity of pride in family and their lives cannot be measured, for of such is built the foundation of a vigorous society.

Chapter 12

Grizzle Bars

Always surprising it is to discover many travelers of Yukon Territory and Alaska have not seen a grizzly bear. Despite environmental disclaimers to the contrary, there appears to be many of these beautiful creatures still prowling about in the North.

The Partridges were intimately familiar with grizzly bears at Bennett City, Millhaven and Ben-My-Chree. They read all they could about them and to that knowledge added their own respect and, it seems likely from Kate Partridge's voluminous diaries, their love.

One cannot speak of Ben-My-Chree without, somewhere along the trail, running into more than a few grizzle bars, both true and fictional. Perhaps you will enjoy a few yarns about them, including one or two which have touched our funny bone. Some we can vouch for, others were related to us by Yukoners whose poker faces revealed not much.

*

On one occasion, three of us were camped on one of the little islands in Deep Bay on Tagish Lake, not far from Golden Gate. We had canoed from Tagish settlement. It was a joy to stretch our legs, pitch the pop-up tent, make a warm brew and explore the isle. Son Russell got out his rod and after a few casts, brought in a good-sized trout which Pat soon had sizzling, and smelled grand. After supper we sat and watched the sun go down behind eternal hills. Peace, content, weary—sleeping bags ahoy.

Early up. Suddenly before breakfast, there was a "wheew-oough!" in a little baylet across the way. Head up and down amidst weeds and water foliage, was a large antlered moose, enjoying a feed. We chattered our surprise and delight. The moose felt that was uncalled for, an intrusion in his kingdom. With annoyed flailing of hoof and head he began to move along the shore through shallows. Those great legs swishing, stomach and furry hide parting lake surface began to make music. Then he was out of sight. But for a long time we heard sounds like a steam train, gathering speed outbound from some far off station. Wheew-wheew-wheew; thump, thump, thump; splash, splash, splash; fading, fading...silence.

The island was only about 100 feet from a lake shore beach, with some twenty feet of sand. "Oh my gosh!" yelled my fisherman son. "There's a bear!" And there was. A grizzly. Ambling along, a little hunched over. In our binoculars he was a sight to remember. Morning light bathed his glossy fur rippling over mighty muscles, legs striding purposefully forward, head weaving ponderously from side to side only a few inches clear of sand.

At first we thought his movements rather slow, but not so. All too soon he was down by the bay's head, disappearing into black alder. Our first ever grizzly, au natural. We felt fearful, vulnerable, awed.

*

Another time we had gone to Carcross to become acquainted with the late George Simmonds and his wife Emily. They lived in a pioneer home backing onto Lake Bennett just about across the street from Matthew Watson's store, and received us graciously. Their weather-beaten home looked its age outside, but was homey inside, replete with comfortable chairs and sofas. There was a piano too, which we learned had been backpacked over the Chilkoot in gold rush days.

Emily brought out tea and home-cooked goodies and we chatted away. George had been an expert dog team driver, delivering mail and freight on the Southern Lakes. He and his wife had known the Partridges well, were familiar with Ben-My-Chree and the story of that wondrous oasis.

We spoke of the rush of Klondike boats from Bennett City right past their back door. And of the railway's arrival in Carcross and on to Whitehorse.

"Y'know Cy," reminisced this cheery Yukon pioneer after he had learned of my 1930s steam boating, "the wife always had ice cold feet. Lordy, this country is cold enough without getting warmed up in bed and then having a couple of icy blocks stuck right in yer gut!

"Well, one day I got to thinkin' maybe a rug on them boards would help a bit; Emily felt the idea was okay an' a bear rug is thick, hairy and warm. I didn't know from Adam's off ox about rifles an' hunting' an' like that, so I went over to the Indian Village 'cross the river and got ahold of Johnny Johns. Johnny was a passin' fair shot and hunted quite a bit. He agreed we should try for a grizzle, or other bear. So we went on out one mornin'. He lent me a spare rifle and took his own. We got up there in the buckbrush and b'gosh there was a sow and her cub.

"'Get back a' that there rock,' said Johnny, 'an' take a bead on the big 'un.' I did, shut my eyes and pulled the trigger. Down she went!

"'By damn,' yelled Johnny. 'Good shot! Now git up thar and catch that cub. Might make a dollar or two, sell him to tha tourists.'

"Now one time some gent told me yer get what they calls buck fever the first time yer knocks down a animal. But I didn't get any of that. I just took a bite of that there sandwich, chewed 'er up, and went phit, phit on the side, like."

Simmonds paused, and looked expectantly at me. Emily just smiled. The seconds ticked by.

"What happened then?" I asked, rather nettled at the delay in what I felt was bound to be a revival of the bear or some other sort of havoc.

"Well," said George, "I may not have had that there buck fever, but I sure above ground forgot to take off the newspaper!"

*

I first met Alan Innes-Taylor while I was centennial commissioner for Yukon in 1967. We were housed in a building close to the hospital across the river from White Pass & Yukon Route rail station in Whitehorse.

Alan was down in the basement. He used to come upstairs and join in with the tourist office staff, my secretary and me for coffee. We found common joy in punning. He liked my thought that the only person who appreciated a pun was someone who could come up with a rip-snorter himself. We got along famously.

One day he invited me home to supper and showed me some photo albums of his early adventures. He had started out as a cabin boy on a Norwegian whaler; had accompanied Admiral Byrd on two trips to the Antarctic, both in charge of sled dogs, once with fifty, later with 300.

He told me a story about those 300 dogs. Byrd's ship *Bear* became a sort of social soiree on her second trip, including amongst the passenger list a soprano of some fame. The *Bear*'s skipper cautioned Taylor, who had the dogs penned on deck, to keep them quiet between seven and nine that night because the lady was going to sing. Alan did his best, hosing down the dogs, giving them extra rations, standing guard with hose and club. Smack on seven, the singer broke forth. Immediately the whole canine company pointed their noses to the moon and howled. Alan was aghast. Nothing would quiet them as long as the warbling went on. He feared the worst come morning.

At 9:30 A.M. the skipper arrived on deck for his regular morning stroll. "Taylor, m'boy, how goes it?" he asked. "Oh yes, about those dogs last night. Between us, I'm mighty glad they were in good voice. That dame certainly was not. The dogs shut her up. She was in a fine pout. They put her to bed with smelling salts. Fine job, son!"

Alan has passed from us now. He was a remarkable man. His life experiences would make a good book. At one time or another he had been a river pilot, mountie, soldier, the only one known to hold a commission in both Canadian and American armies at the same time, while offering himself as a guinea pig in an experiment to discover whether bovine encephalomyelitis was infectious to humans. As a researcher in Arctic and Antarctic survival, he proved a communal sleeping bag housing five survivors produced the maximum warmth possible, while six or more resulted in less per person.

He was employed for a period of time as an historian by both Yukon Territorial and Canadian federal governments. His labors recorded and resulted in the restoration of many historically valuable sites and buildings throughout Yukon. Other talents included organizing and promoting the Dawson tent festival. He authored many unpublished papers on Yukon history.

"Grizzly bears," he told me one day, "are magnificent. Why anyone would want to shoot one is beyond me. Stupid, uncivilized, awful! Out with them! I was on a bit of a tramp once and I came up over a little hill. Down in the valley beyond were five grizzlies chewing away on a moose."

"Five!" I said. "What did you do?"

"Simple," replied the inimitable Yukoner. "I just turned myself about and gave them one more trail to follow!"

*

We have told of our affection for the Brook family at "Brooklands." They have some lovely bear yarns, one of which really tickles me pink. They did not relate this one to us, but two different people have vouched for it.

For years Marion, a dainty little dame notwithstanding rifle and trapping skills, fishing, wood-chopping, etc., pleaded with Reg, her late husband, to let her order a plastic seat for the outhouse. For a long, long time she had put up with a splintery wooden perch. Reg, who had steered his pioneer family through the depression, mainly by running a tight ship, pointed out that an outhouse seat was just that, no more, no less. Request denied. However, at last he relented; out came the Sears catalogue. The pink treasure arrived in due time and was installed.

One spring morning about 3:00 A.M., there was a sizable noise in the general direction of the Brookland's outhouse. Reg leapt up, grabbed a rifle, and tore out the back door in his long-johns, cranking in a shell as he went. The outhouse was taking a fearsome beating by an angry grizzle sow. The door, which opened inward, was jammed shut. Terrified howls, squeals and thumps emitted. The sounds told Reg one scared cub had somehow gotten in, backed himself against the door and could not get out. Ma bear was getting madder by the moment. Finally, she dealt the structure a horrendous clout. Out shot wee bear, howling a storm, the precious pink seat around his neck. Away up the trail he ran, mother close behind.

That was the last anyone saw of Marion's prize plastic seat!

*

Not far north of "Brooklands" and Golden Gate is a little baylet facing toward Whitehorse. Pat and I had been in Harder's Ten-Mile

Ranch for yet another load of partition logs and two-by-ten rough boards to floor our new log cabin at Ben-My. Worn out with loading and a long day, we put into Port Royale for supper. We should have stayed there for the night, but I was anxious to push on. Days were slipping past and the cabin needed finishing. So we set out across the lake and up a few miles toward Brook's. It began to darken and blow a bit. Into the nearest bay on one of several islands we went. I angled one of the barge pontoons onto a shallow beach with brush about a foot back from the water.

Our barge was heavily loaded with logs and planks plus a forty-five-gallon drum of gas, and other gear. Had the load not been mostly wood, we would have hesitated to carry so much weight, resulting in little freeboard.

After a hot drink and supper ashore using the Coleman gas stove, we built a rough log platform for sleeping bags and air mattresses on the same pontoon side moored ashore. Then we climbed out of feather jackets and got ready to snuggle in. Pat was already tucked in with toque and wooly scarf, only nose and eye showing. I bundled up my jacket for a pillow, stripped down to a red flannel shirt and b.v.d.s, put one foot inside the bag when there came two sounds from shore which virtually froze my blood! The first was a series of childlike whimpers from brush dead ahead. The second, the most horrendous bellowing roars combined with thrashing, banging and breaking of wood not more than fifty feet to the left.

Individual hairs stood up on the back of my neck. I scrambled over Pat, got into what we called our cabin, a small plywood structure astern, grabbed my rifle and a clip of shells, and stood beside Pat's bed, cranking in a cartridge. The roaring got louder, whimpers too. It was rapidly getting dark. During all this I had come to the conclusion that what we had to contend with was a grizzly sow and a cub or two. Likely we were smack in between the two parties. Even as a comparative bear novice, I knew that was less than good. I let go a shot from the hip at the center of that roaring.

I prepared to let go another shot, this time from shoulder level, carefully aiming in the now dark, for what I judged to be hopefully a vital grizzly part. Then it suddenly dawned on me that might not be too bright. I could not see the bear, but she probably could see me. We were vulnerable.

The whimpers sounded a bit more anxious, roaring and branch breaking a lot louder. I sprang ashore, grabbed the Coleman, lost the grate, yanked the mooring rope from a bush and leaped back aboard the barge. That was a bad move. The unbalanced barge, now free of a stabilizing pontoon formerly on shore, tipped alarmingly, nearly putting Pat's head into the lake. My precious feather jacket fell overboard.

We began, thank goodness, to rapidly drift broadside down the bay. We had always tied up nights ashore, so no anchor. For a fellow who had owned a fleet of power boats in order to sell and develop British Columbia oceanfront properties, this was embarrassing. However, I did have a brand new metal tool case full of socket wrenches and other treasured tools. It only took a moment to whip on a bowline and overboard. How, I'll never know, but the case wedged itself behind a rock below and held. We hung there in a bit of a chop, not quite on the main lake. The whimpering, now faint, slowly moved toward mother. Bit by bit, the noise subsided. What was left moved away from our bay. Silence, except for wind and wave. We did not sleep a wink. About four the next morning we weighed anchor, fired up the outboard and left as fast as possible, and shaped course for Brooklands.

Over coffee and stacks of hot cakes, Reg Brook, an experienced trapper, looked somewhat scornfully at us, smiled and fetched himself yet another cup of Yukon tea, the kind that soon destroys silver or even stainless steel spoons. In his eyes, we Porters were, on a scale of one to ten, about a two.

"Y'know Cy, the head of that bay is one of the largest cross-lake game trails 'round here. What you had was a grizzle all right, and cubs. You're lucky to be alive!"

I know.

*

Up at Ben-My-Chree we had put the finishing touches to our new log cabin. A delightfully comfy queen-sized bed was set up in the front room. From it we could look through out large front windows across the meadows and beach down toward the beach and lake.

Pat had often said how she would love to see an outstanding display of northern lights. One night, about 2:00 A.M., I woke up to see the sky alive with summer aura borealis. I woke Pat and got her to the windows. We stood there marveling as swaths of shimmering colors moved across the lake from mountain to mountain and back again. It was superb.

"Why not go outside where we can see the whole sky?" I asked.

"You bet!" agreed an entranced wife.

Now we never went outside after dark because we knew from time to time grizzlies passed through the property. Once, when geological students from Oshkosh University were camped in the old homestead building, their leader, Professor Tom Laudon, was taking his ease in a chair outside after supper. To his amazement and considerable awe, a large grizzly sow, followed by two cubs, ambled right through the encampment within ten feet of the teacher and a few of his students. So we had been careful.

But this night, out we went anyway, determined to make the most of a stunning show. It was a night not to be missed. The day before I had been repairing a tin chimney on a storage shed about twenty feet away from our new cabin. I had left a ladder leaning against the shed. We stood together, leaning against the ladder, facing the lake, where the lights were at their best.

Suddenly there was a long drawn out scratch on the ladder about hip high. Frozen fear! The scratch came higher. There was a fetid hot breath. Some hair brushed my ear, then coarse whiskers passed across my face. Deep breathing. We stood rigid. It had to be a bear!

A cold wet nose pushed into my ear, followed by a well-known "Meow!"

It was our Siamese cat...

Epilogue

By 1987 we had shifted our barge from McLeod's at Tagish to Brooklands on Graham Arm. Bea and George were about to sell and retire to Whitehorse, closer to the amenities. Our new move was designed to have Jim Brook care for the rig and outboard engine. In return he could make use of the gear to haul in supplies. The arrangement worked well.

About this time my wife and I began to realize we would shortly reach a point in our lives where the long and expensive trek North would be difficult, perhaps impractical. I was entering my sixty-fifth year. Our ocean-oriented realty and sister development companies had been sold or stood down. We thought it would be a good idea to bring forth a book about Ben-My-Chree. But one more thing was rattling around in the upper story.

For years I had cherished the idea of reactivating visitor traffic on those beautiful Southern Lakes. Visions of refurbishing *Tutshi* with help from White Pass & Yukon Route, cruise lines, air carriers and tour companies became a sizable portion of my thoughts. Once we had published a tourist magazine, *Alaska Traveler*, distributing it on major tourist routes and carriers. Most aspects of the visitor industry were familiar to us. Would we somehow be the ones to get things rolling again, notwithstanding the short season? About this time we received a phone call from a friend in eastern Canada whose government branch had helped us with financing for a precut housing agency. He told us there was a feasibility study under way to access reactivation of visitor traffic on the Lakes. Perhaps Ben-My would blossom once more.

We traced the promoter to Whitehorse. He was a former bus tour operator, trying to raise funds to build and operate a 250-passenger power catamaran based on an Australian design. Nothing came of his plan to launch at Carcross or the old Conrad on Windy Arm, build a lodge and cottages at Ben-My and acquire Kirkland's Resort in Atlin, re-establishing the old circular water route. It was exciting to find ideas like these circulating. Sooner or later the potential for visitors on these waterways would result in positive action. A passenger catamaran suddenly appeared at Dawson, transporting visitors up and down the Yukon River to Circle, Alaska, with alternate bus connections.

Was it possible a modern version of the old Tutshi cruises was, like the paddlewheelers of old, just around the bend? Would hundreds of astonished travelers behold our oasis of international peace in the wilderness again? Surely a benevolent spirit stood watch over this special place, anxious to share a beauty beyond compare.

Once upon a time there had been a young man waiting on table, serving the well-to-do, marveling with them at the cultivated flowers, fountains, wishing wells, rimmed by sunset-garnished mounts and a brooding glacier. In those days, youthful imagination and yearnings had reached their apex in a North, once part of Yukon Territory, where the first tricklings of snow water signaled the beginnings of a mighty watershed and river. The dream of ownership had come to pass. That mystical golden thread still vibrated among the peaks.

Yet it was not to be; at least not on our watch. So Pat and I and Nui-Nui, our cat, continued each year on our way to Ben-My-Chree. Often we encountered stiff, jarring waves. Hours later, cold, tired and not too happy, we came to the end on the lake, and decided to do some careful thinking. We resolved either to pass the place to our children, or to sell. We called a family conference back home. What did the family wish us to do? We all faced a difficult decision. After two heartfelt sessions with contributions from children and their mates, we reluctantly concluded that to turn Ben-My over to our younger generation would present them with a burden rather than a benefit. They had generously contributed to Dad's dream and in the doing become part of a fine adventure. Now priorities pointed in other directions. Even if we were to set up a reserve foundation to cover fixed annual costs, it was doubtful if the young generation would find time and travel dollars to regularly visit, maintain and enjoy Ben-My. So we would sell.

In Victoria I had a friend, Bryan McGill, editor of *Beautiful British Columbia*, whose magazine was just starting to accept advertising, having switched to private enterprise. At that time their back cover was available. I purchased the page, and since Ben-My-Chree was a rather romantic saga, we managed a four-page color picture article inside. Such was the circulation and interest in the magazine, that shortly thereafter inquiries began to come in. It was a difficult place to sell, far off and expensive to show. Eventually, however, we found the right chap, and a sale was completed. The new owner would create a game reserve, letting the bears, moose, goats and so on prowl about at their leisure.

Our plans for a book you have now read, and I hope enjoyed. During research I realized all our family had experienced something more than admiration for the beauty and history of Ben-My-Chree. My eldest daughter Kerrie accompanied me on a final session in Whitehorse at the Territorial Archives. We were winding up notes and photographs on the last day before flying out, when an archivist drew my attention to a recent folio on the Ben-My access file. "It's just a few general notes," said she, "likely you already know all about it."

Normally, I would have ignored any more detail. After all, the book had been paddling along for more than twelve years.

But something, perhaps that same golden thread, had one more secret to impart. I asked Kerrie to take a look. A few minutes later she returned, and through more than one tear, whispered, "Dad, you're not going to believe this!" I looked at the folio, which contained a few notes on the Partridges, details of birth, death, marriage and so forth. The last line stated Kate's maiden name: Pridham.

At age ten in Alberni, upon death of my birth mother, breakdown and subsequent passing of my father in England, I had been taken in by Reverend R. D. Porter, a Church of England clergyman and his wife Vivian. Loved, fed, cared for and schooled, in gratitude I had changed my birth name to theirs overseas during World War II, becoming a Porter. My birth name had been Pridham!

Otto Partridge had married his cousin Kate. I was related in some way to The Lady of the Lake, the Girl of My Heart, and her husband. What a way to write finish to an adventure, and to this book. All the family had been singularly blessed during our northern sojourn. We had fallen under the spell of the Yukon like many others. Happy memories fill our hearts. The dream of long ago had come true.

The quest for Ben-My-Chree is complete. In the words of Robert
W. Service:

Here by the campfire's flicker,
Deep in my blanket curled,
I long for the peace of the pine-gloom
When the scroll of the Lord is unfurled,
And the wind and the wave are silent,
And world is singing to world.

It is to be content.

MORE GREAT HANCOCK HOUSE TITLES

Native Titles

Ah Mo
Tren J. Griffin
ISBN 0-88839-244-3

American Indian Pottery
Sharon Wirt
ISBN 0-88839-134-X

Argillite: Art of the Haida
Drew & Wilson
ISBN 0-88839-037-8

Art of the Totem
Marius Barbeau
ISBN 0-88839-168-4

Coast Salish
Reg Ashwell
ISBN 0-88839-009-2

End of Custer
Dale T. Schoenberger
ISBN 0-88839-288-5

Eskimo Life Yesterday
Hancock House
ISBN 0-919654-73-8

Guide to Indian Quillworking
Christy Ann Hensler
ISBN 0-88839-214-1

Haida: Their Art & Culture
Leslie Drew
ISBN 0-88839-132-3

Hunter Series
R. Stephen Irwin, MD,
Illustrations J. B. Clemens:

Hunters of the Buffalo
ISBN 0-88839-176-5

Hunters of the E. Forest
ISBN 0-88839-178-1

Hunters of the Ice
ISBN 0-88839-179-X

Hunters of the N. Forest
ISBN 0-88839-175-7

Hunters of the Sea
ISBN 0-88839-177-3

Images: Stone: B.C.
Wilson Duff
ISBN 0-295-95421-3

Indian Herbs
Dr. Raymond Stark
ISBN 0-88839-077-7

Indian Tribes of the NW
Reg Ashwell
ISBN 0-919654-53-3

Iroquois: Their Art & Crafts
Carrie A. Lyford
ISBN 0-88839-135-8

Kwakiutl Art & Culture
Reg Ashwell
ISBN 0-88839-325-3

More Ah Mo
Tren J. Griffin
ISBN 0-88839-231-1

My Heart Soars
Chief Dan George
ISBN 0-88839-231-1

MORE GREAT HANCOCK HOUSE TITLES

My Spirit Soars
Chief Dan George
ISBN 0-88839-233-8

NW Native Harvest
Carol Batdorf
ISBN 0-88839-245-1

Power Quest
Carol Batdorf
ISBN 0-88839-240-0

Spirit Quest
Carol Batdorf
ISBN 0-88839-210-9

Tlingit: Art, Culture &
Legends
Dan & Nan Kaiper
ISBN 0-88839-101-6

Totem Poles of the NW
D. Allen
ISBN 0-919654-83-5

When Buffalo Ran
George Bird Grinnell
ISBN 0-88839-258-3

Northern Biographies

Bootlegger's Lady
Sager & Frye
ISBN 0-88839-976-6

Crazy Cooks & Gold
Miners
Joyce Yardley
ISBN 0-88839-294-X

Descent into Madness
Vernon Frolick
ISBN 0-88839-300-8

Fogswamp: Life with Swans
Turner & McVeigh
ISBN 0-88839-104-8

Lady Rancher
Gertrude Roger
ISBN 0-88839-099-8

Nahanni
Dick Turner
ISBN 0-88839-028-9

Novice in the North
Bill Robinson
ISBN 0-88839-977-4

Ralph Edwards of
Lonesome Lake
Ed Gould
ISBN 0-88839-100-5

Ruffles on my Longjohns
Isabel Edwards
ISBN 0-88839-102-1

Wings of the North
Dick Turner
ISBN 0-88839-060-2

Yukon Lady
Hugh McLean
ISBN 0-88839-186-2

Yukoners
Harry Gordon-Cooper
ISBN 0-88839-232-X